CANNERY ROW

THE HISTORY OF OLD OCEAN VIEW AVENUE

By

MICHAEL KENNETH HEMP

FIRST EDITION

Published by
THE HISTORY COMPANY
Monterey

Printed in "Steinbeck Country" by
K/P GRAPHICS
Salinas

THE HISTORY COMPANY
P.O. Box 1882
Monterey, California 93942
(408) 375-3882

Printed in the United States of America

10 9 8 7 6 5 4 3 2 1

LIBRARY OF CONGRESS CATALOGING-IN-PUBLICATION DATA

Hemp, Michael Kenneth, 1942-
     Cannery Row: the history of old ocean view avenue

     Bibliography: p.
     Includes index.
     1. Cannery Row (Monterey, Calif.) 2. Monterey (Calif.)—History.
     3. Steinbeck, John, 1902-1968—Homes and haunts—California—Monterey.
I. Title.
F869.M7H35   1986   979.4'76   86-32023

ISBN 0-941425-00-2

Book and Cover Design by Robert Wiles Edison and Michael K. Hemp
Typography by Elaine Funchess-Jones, Monterey
Production by K/P Graphics, Salinas
Distribution by THE HISTORY COMPANY

THIS BOOK IS DEDICATED TO THE CANNERY ROW "ALUMNI" — THE MEN AND WOMEN WHO WORKED ITS CANNERIES AND THE MEN WHO BRAVED THE PACIFIC FOR ITS SILVER HARVEST.

Cover Photo:

Pacific Fish Company crew, 1911.

Photo courtesy Charles Nonella, whose parents both appear in this photo of Cannery Row's first major cannery.

THE PHOTOGRAPHY IN THIS BOOK
IS AVAILABLE FROM THE
PAT HATHAWAY
HISTORICAL PHOTO COLLECTION
OF CALIFORNIA VIEWS

763 Lighthouse Avenue
Monterey, California 93940
(408) 373-3811

The 60,000 images in this historical photo collection include Monterey, Carmel, Pacific Grove, Pebble Beach, Carmel Valley, Big Sur, California missions, and the San Francisco earthquake and fire.

The Hathaway Collection Catalog Number is indicated in brackets on each photo contained in this book. Inquiries for photo reproductions or enlargements must be accompanied by the catalog number.

THE PHOTOGRAPHERS

SPECIAL THANKS

My Special Thanks go to the following people, without whom there would likely be no such book, now or perhaps ever:

Charles Nonella, Frank Wright, Pat Hathaway, Horace "Sparky" Enea, Skipper Tony Berry, Tom Mangelsdorf, William B. Brown, Ed Ricketts, Jr., Fred Strong, Joanna Livesay and Ten Bears, Will Shaw and The Thomas Doud Sr. and Anita M. Doud Fund of the Community Foundation for Monterey County, The Board of Directors of The Cannery Row Foundation, Skipper Salvatore Enea, Skipper Horace Balbo, Betty Hoag McGlynn, Mrs. Wesley Dodge, Skipper James Davi, Frank and Grace Bergara, Al and Esther Campoy, Dorothy Wheeler, Beth Robinson, Eldon Dedini, Tom Weber, Antonette Villines, Ray "Spats" Lucido, Robert Enea, Ted Melicia, Frank Tanaka, John Gota, Seizo Kodani, Francisco "Paco" Ferro, Maury Cooper, Bernard Jaksha, Frank Crispo, Daryl Stokes, John Stidham, Kalisa Moore, Dick O'Kane, Michael Maiorana, Frank Dobronte, Anna Nowak and the Paquin Family, Anne-Marie Hemp, David Hemp, Sally Hemp, Terri Wolfson, Robert Edison, Dave Davis, Bob Lippi and Chuck Sievers of K/P Graphics ... and all the Cannery Workers, Skippers and Fishermen who have assisted this research. None of this could have happened without the Cannery Row Foundation and its donor members.

TABLE OF CONTENTS

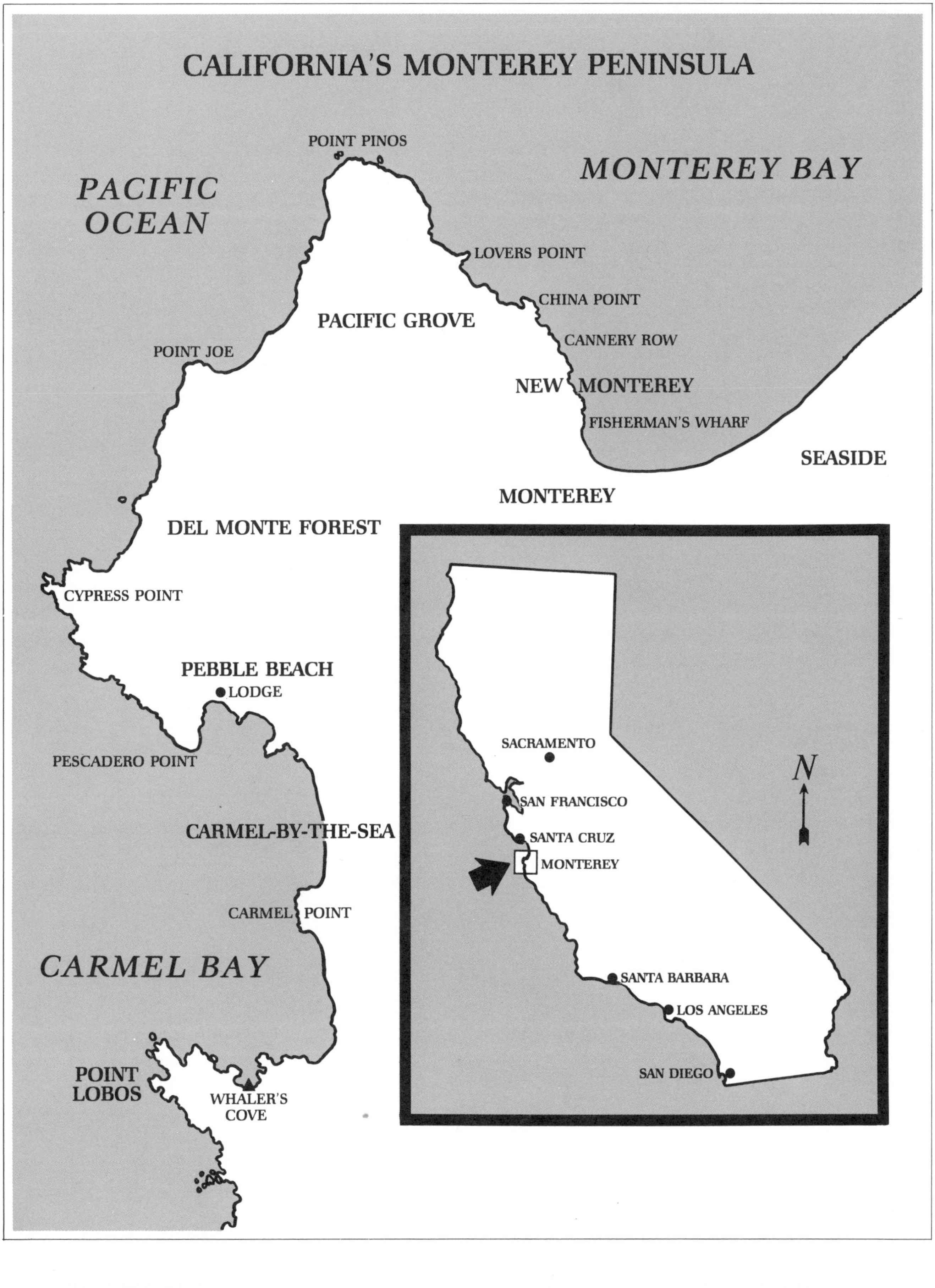

CALIFORNIA'S MONTEREY PENINSULA

PACIFIC OCEAN

MONTEREY BAY

POINT PINOS

LOVERS POINT

PACIFIC GROVE

CHINA POINT

CANNERY ROW

POINT JOE

NEW MONTEREY

FISHERMAN'S WHARF

SEASIDE

MONTEREY

DEL MONTE FOREST

CYPRESS POINT

PEBBLE BEACH
●LODGE

PESCADERO POINT

CARMEL-BY-THE-SEA

CARMEL POINT

CARMEL BAY

POINT LOBOS

WHALER'S COVE

SACRAMENTO

SAN FRANCISCO

SANTA CRUZ

MONTEREY

N

SANTA BARBARA

LOS ANGELES

SAN DIEGO

AUTHOR'S NOTES

Two of Cannery Row's most notable personalities have inspired the concept and design of this book: John Steinbeck and his close friend and mentor, Edward F. "Doc" Ricketts. John Steinbeck's *Cannery Row* is a concise and easily read account of life on old Ocean View Avenue in the 1930's, focusing on the adventures of his friend "Doc" and the misadventures of one of the most colorful casts of characters in American literature. John's interest and concern for the human touch in his fiction left little room, however, for facts that did not serve his nostalgic imagery.

Marine biologist Ed Ricketts loved "true things" and he pursued his controversial approach to the study of marine biology with an awareness of how important *context* is in the discovery, explanation and understanding of physical, biological phenomena. His pioneering study of the inter-relationship of the organisms in the tide pools of the intertidal zone — the specialty which he came to know and understand so well — provided the model for approaching all subjects.

CANNERY ROW The History of Old Ocean View Avenue is therefore concise, human and graphic, as John would like it. It is also as precise as current available research can make it. Its scope is intentionally broad enough to include the *context* of Monterey history necessary for an understanding and appreciation of the time and place the world has come to know as Cannery Row. I think that Ed Ricketts would further appreciate its utility in that this book — with its photography from the Pat Hathaway Historical Photo Collection and the detailed map-guide to old Ocean View Avenue — will prove especially useful to those with the opportunity to seek Cannery Row's history and the romantic nostalgia of its Steinbeck legacy in person.

Cannery Row would certainly have an historical identity of its own on the dubious merits of the ecological and economic disaster resulting from the collapse of the sardine fishery and the major Monterey industry it supported. But the men and women of the 1930's and 1940's that became subjects of John Steinbeck's *Cannery Row* have provided the nostalgic focal point for the whole of Monterey's canning history. The literary success of *Cannery Row* has elevated the street to world fame through John's wry and compassionate accounts of its "human condition," drawn largely from direct observation and participation in the decade of the thirties.

A primary objective of this book is to provide a vision of The Row as it was, from which unfolds both its emerging but little known "human history" and a vivid background for John Steinbeck's fiction. The map-guide and its indexed historical and Steinbeck landmarks serves to prepare or supplement the reading of the following books relating to Cannery Row by John Steinbeck:

Cannery Row, 1945

Sweet Thursday, the sequel to *Cannery Row*, 1954

Log From the Sea of Cortez, 1951 — containing the "About Ed Ricketts" preface to the restructured 1941 publication of *Sea of Cortez*, co-authored by John Steinbeck and Edward F. Ricketts.

With or without such preparation, however, this presentation of Monterey's fishing and canning history provides a new and vivid perspective designed to enhance your appreciation and enjoyment of Cannery Row, particularly as less and less remains of the Old Row. With this book and the magic of your imagination you are invited to adventure into Cannery Row. It will never be again as it was, but the future will somehow always hold its ghost.

—*MICHAEL HEMP*

In this earliest known photo of the coastal road that was to become Ocean View Avenue, the rocks of China Point in the distance

INTRODUCTION

Cannery Row's origins are a mixture of the rocky Monterey coastline and the toil and industry of the Orient. A Chinese fishing village, from which "China Point" derives its name, was established in the early 1850's and was devastated by fire in 1906.

Monterey's first major canning operation had begun next to Fisherman's Wharf when F.E. Booth's sardine canning experiment was matched with the skill of Sicilian fishermen and "lampara" fishing techniques. Booth's early development of sardine packing depended on innovative and inventive personnel, many of whom went on to own or operate other canneries — all of which were forced to locate away from the harbor, along a rocky stretch of coastline out toward the Chinatown near Pacific Grove.

The rutty, unpaved coastal road from Monterey to Pacific Grove grew to host the sardine factories that for half a century would dominate Monterey history and commerce. In 1902, Harry Malpas founded the first canning operation on Ocean View Avenue. In 1958 the street was renamed "Cannery Row" in honor of a writer who few regarded seriously when he had frequented it: John Steinbeck.

The intervening years are an epic tale of the lives, labor and fortunes at stake on Ocean View Avenue in the plunder of a seemingly inexhaustible natural resource — sardines.

Two World Wars, Prohibition and the Great Depression imprinted their marks on this famous street and its "Alumni." Fate's greatest imprint was cast with the disappearance of the sardines in the late 1940's. Depletion of the fishery, currents and pollution in the food chain have all been

mark the origin of Monterey's fishing industry.

C.W.J. Johnson photo, early 1880's. [75-06-4]

blamed for the demise of this once major industry and the street that supported it.

Ed "Doc" Ricketts' famous comment, "They're all in cans" is an admitted oversimplification. Of course, he and other authorities on the fishery knew only too well the other answer, with roots even deeper in the canning process: two thirds of Monterey's sardines never made it into cans at all. They left town on the Southern Pacific rails as 100 lb. sacks of fishmeal and as sardine oil. The *reduction process* which turned the silver tide into sardine by-products was far more profitable than canning for consumption, which required a much larger labor force and sold in far less profitable markets.

By the end of the forties, decades of warnings and urgent appeals for conservation had been ignored, ridiculed and discredited. Wartime patriotic fervor had also done little to encourage either conservation or attention to what scientists like Ed Ricketts knew only too well: Cannery Row was about to commit suicide.

The sardines virtually vanished by the early fifties. The last sardine catch was packed in 1964, with the last operating cannery, the Hovden Food Products Corporation — now the Monterey Bay Aquarium — closing its doors forever in 1973 ... canning squid.

The ecological disaster was, of course, mirrored by pain and human suffering as Monterey's major commercial resource mysteriously disappeared, leaving the once thriving fishing and canning industry to die on its waterfront in a ghostly gray demise. There was a time, however, when the inhabitants of this coast were far less vulnerable and dependent on the *commercial* bounty from the sea. And that is where *this* story of Cannery Row really begins ... .

FIRST INHABITANTS

It may have been the place the tribes called "Tamokt," the grassy hill overlooking the rocky hook at the south end of the long beach. To the north was the slough country, now known as Elkhorn, which provided fish, waterfowl and game for their diet, as its river wandered in wide marshes to the sea. These gentle, primitive natives were scattered in small groups along the shore and throughout the coastal and inland valleys. Their nomadic food-gathering and hunting took them wherever the seasonal foraging, game and weather provided them refuge and provision.

It is likely that from this spot the Indians witnessed Captain Juan Cabrillo's passing in November 1542, unable to anchor due to a severe storm. The expedition of Sebastian Viscaino, which anchored in the bay December 5, 1602, was to claim this land for Spain — to include its "Costanoan" subjects.

Seasonal movements, acorn gathering, hunting and shellfish collecting continued uninterrupted until the Spanish came again in 1770, this time bringing Father Serra by sea, to meet Gaspar de Portola's overland detachment that had marched north from San Diego. The meeting point of these two expeditions was where the small creek ran into the bay, below the Costanoan knoll. This time the white men stayed and forever changed the fate of Monterey Bay's hapless original inhabitants. It also signaled the end of man's use of the bounty of this sea for his subsistence. The new lords of this coast were to set in motion the commercial use of its resources, a concept alien to the Costanoan except for the shiny shells they traded to inland tribes.

In the century to follow, these passive "savages" were evangelized, exploited, dispersed, decimated by white men's diseases and racially absorbed into the Spanish and Mexican populations. Their vantage point above the bay had, however, quickly become the site of the conquistador's "presidio."

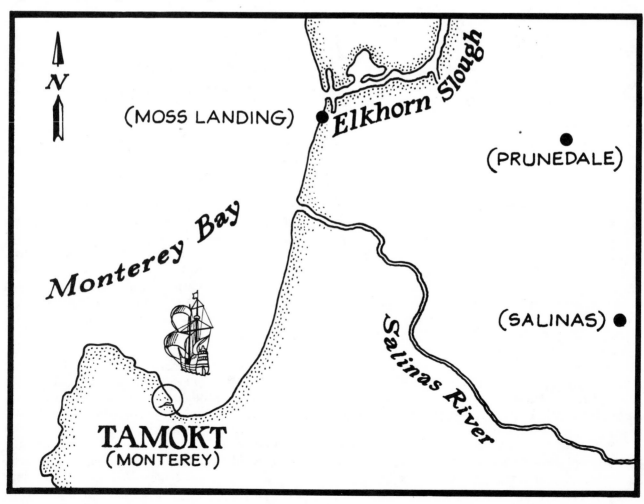

A VIEW FROM THE PRESIDIO

In the years since Serra's landing, the knoll that was once the sight of the Costanoan "rancheria" was to witness the establishment of Monterey as the Spanish capital of Alta California and the construction of "El Castillo," a fort at its crest with a view to the sea and the sprawling cluster of early structures on its shoreline.

In November 1818, three years before Mexican independence, the fort and harbor were brought under siege by the Argentine pirate Hippolite Bouchard. The town was looted and burned before his two ships set sail, the fortress having failed its protective purpose.

New England whaling ships were a common sight at anchor to replenish their provisions. The Alta California coastline was also familiar with Russian otter hunters, employing Aleuts with sealskin boats, who were joined by Spanish and American hunters to bring this widely pursued Pacific Coast species to near extinction, ironically about the time Charles Darwin was penning *The Origin of Species*.

On July 7, 1846, Commodore John Drake Sloat was to bring California under the flag of the United States when his forces put ashore to hoist the American flag at the Custom House. The Americans immediately set out to construct their own defenses on the knoll, known as Fort Mervine. Then came the gold rush to the Sierras which nearly shut Monterey down, even closing the fort in 1852. Reactivated briefly during the Civil War, it remained unused from 1865 to 1902.

The distant Hotel Del Monte, its beachside bath house, Monterey's train depot, and the Pacific Coast Steamship Co. pier share the view from the former Costanoan knoll.   C.W.J. Johnson photo, early 1880's. [75-06-15]

THE POINT PINOS LIGHTHOUSE

The first navigation aids for west coast shipping were approved by Congress in 1850 which allocated funds for the construction of a series of eight lighthouses on the Pacific Coast — one located at Point Pinos, now Pacific Grove. The completed lighthouse cast its beacon for the first time on February 1, 1855, its lard oil light source replaced by kerosene in 1880, and by electricity in 1915.

Its first light keeper, Charles Layton, was killed in its first year of operation while on a posse in pursuit of Anastacio Garcia, one of the Central Coast's most notorious outlaws. Two of its light keepers have been women: Layton's widow, Charlotte, and Mrs. Emily A. Fish, 1893.

This beacon is now a Pacific Grove landmark, open for tours, and the longest continuously operating lighthouse on the West Coast. Only San Francisco's Alcatraz light is older, but has not operated continuously. [72-08-72]

PACIFIC GROVE

In 1875, a year after the arrival of rail service to the Monterey Peninsula, Reverend J.W. Ross formed the Pacific Grove Retreat Association, establishing a Methodist Episcopal Retreat in the wooded slopes above Point Pinos. Originally a summer tent camp, in 1889 its permanent residents incorporated Pacific Grove, complete with a curfew law and a fence that surrounded the entire settlement. Its gate was locked each night until Judge Langford, a prominent attorney, tired of the long walk for its key and chopped it down. It was never replaced.

The growth of the town soon made it an adversary of the continued Chinese occupation at China Point. In addition to the repulsive smell of drying fish and squid from the settlement, the righteous Christians of Pacific Grove became increasingly agitated over their "heathen" religious ceremonies and unorthodox customs — such as the smoking of opium. Additionally, the Southern Pacific's acquisition of huge tracts of Monterey, Pacific Grove and Carmel Bay real estate included prime shoreline property envisioned for development — including China Point. Bolstered by resentment and public opinion against the Chinese, in 1905 its Pacific Improvement Company ordered them off the site which they had been leasing since the 1850's.

The Methodist summer tent cabins established with the arrival of rail service to the Peninsula soon gave way to a real town in the piney woods above Point Pinos. C.W.J. Johnson photo, early 1880's. [78-06-1]

THE CHINESE

Few peoples on earth use more of everything they catch, grow or process than do the Chinese; virtually nothing is wasted. So it was that when the first Chinese settled in the Monterey Bay area — in the cove at Point Lobos about 1851 — they must have rejoiced at the variety and bounty offered to their talents as experienced fishermen.

Sandy Lydon's brilliant work on the Chinese of the Monterey Bay region, *Chinese Gold*, is quick to point out that the Chinese settlements at Point Lobos, "China Point" (near Cannery Row), and Pescadero (Stillwater Cove) were populated by fishing *families*, often having arrived directly by junk from China. Unlike other early groups immigrating to the Monterey Bay, the Chinese came as whole families and took up fishing for their own subsistence, and for drying and shipment to other Chinese enclaves in America or export to China.

Monterey's fishing industry was established by the industrious Chinese who brought with them the technique of preserving their catch by drying it for shipment, an important element in the development of this major industry made possible by Monterey's dependably dry summer months. Not since the Costanoans had anyone used the total environmental resources so thoroughly, but unfortunately the efficiency with which they did so raised both concern and an element of envy among their many critics. With a purported $200,000 annual business at the turn of the century, the Chinese became the target for more than simple racial intolerance; their diversity and adaptation to the marine resources unexploited by European immigrants led the more resourceful of those groups into direct competition with them.

The growth of Monterey's Chinese community in the late 1800's was paralleled by the influx of European immigrants, most notably the Italians, who took up fishing as their major commercial activity. Early struggles for primacy left the Chinese to adjust to the rapid success of Italian companies using the railhead to San Francisco to market "fresh" fish from their operations near the Customs House.

Restrictive legislation and regulation of Chinese fishing and processing techniques, and rising anti-Chinese sentiment, pressured the adaptive Orientals into a commercial species not in conflict with the rapidly entrenched Italian

An early but unknown photographer records the Chinese settlement, its Joss House, and a junk anchored offshore. The odor from drying fish and squid was not a problem in the initial isolation of their settlement.   [72-17-130]

fishermen: squid. It was not a commodity of concern to European immigrant fishing groups and had the advantage of being conducted *at night*, when their fishing operations did not conflict with their rival's use of the bay. Pacific Grove's "Feast of Lanterns" is a tribute to the torches and pitch-wood fires used from the Chinese sampans to attract the curious squid to their waiting seines.

Exclusionary legislation heavily restricting Chinese immigration, prohibiting naturalization, ownership of land, testimony against whites, and access to public education, provided the backdrop against which local forces were being brought to bear: they were no longer welcome on China Point.

Regardless of actual cause, on the evening of May 16, 1906, the Chinatown where Pacific Grove borders New Monterey, was engulfed in flames that destroyed nearly the entire shanty-like settle-ment — itself hosting refugees from the April 18 San Francisco earthquake and fire. This pyre signalled the end of the Chinese fishing industry. Within a year its undispersed inhabitants negotiated for and relocated to a new and much smaller settlement on McAbee Beach on Ocean View Avenue, near the center of what was to become "Cannery Row."

One of the few structures to survive the fire was the Joss House, or shrine. Perhaps only Trinity County's Weaverville Joss House rivals it in significance. Unfortunately, unlike its Weaverville counterpart, it did not achieve preservation as an historical monument. After the fire, it was moved to McAbee Beach where it remained until the late 1920's. In the early 1940's it was torn down on a lot shared with a triplex for single cannery workers, known by its inhabitants and neighbors as the "Palace Flophouse."

This view from the beach shows the flat-bottomed Chinese fishing boats and a portion of their shanty-like village. Nothing remains of this scene except the rock protruding from the buildings on the right. [72-08-132]

The drying of fish and squid was a process of major importance in the Chinese fishing industry. Drying racks and the open fields around the village were routinely used for this purpose.   C.E. Watkins photo, 1883. [78-50-1]

This photo was taken after 1889, when the Southern Pacific tracks to Pacific Grove bisected the village site. The settlement's cemetery is seen at the crest of the hill behind the village.   [80-07-1]

The main street of Chinatown before the May 16, 1906 fire, with the settlement's prominent granite landmark rising above the roofs of the Chinese village. [78-37-1]

The nearly same view of the street after the inferno with guards to prevent the Chinese from rebuilding their burned-out and looted village. A relief fund of $27 was collected for the displaced Chinese. [81-62-14]

WHAT A DIFFERENCE A TRAIN MAKES

The original trackway laid the nearly twenty miles between Salinas and Monterey in 1874, built largely by Chinese labor, was a "Granger's" challenge to the rail freight monopoly of the "Big Four" — Crocker, Stanford, Huntington and Hopkins. It was a narrow-gauge system connecting the Salinas wheat and agricultural markets to a rail pier in Monterey for shipment by sea. It also enabled the growing Monterey fishing industry to connect to major markets for its "fresh" fish up the line and in San Francisco. The Italian and Portuguese operators in Monterey did not ice or eviscerate (gut) the catch for shipment; the waste in spoiled fish kept the prices up.

Although the Monterey & Salinas Valley Railroad failed within five years — primarily due to winter bridge failures over the Salinas River — it demonstrated the market it could serve and its valuable access to the scenic Monterey Peninsula, which was quickly targeted for development as a resort destination.

When Southern Pacific bought the bankrupt railroad at auction, it matched the acquisition with a purchase of 7,000 acres of prime land on the peninsula from David Jacks, to complement and support Crocker's dream of constructing "the most elegant seaside establishment in the world." The doorway to the Monterey Bay area had been opened to tourism and large scale land development.

The iron horses of Southern Pacific brought the wealthy to the Hotel Del Monte and immigrants—notably the Italians—to the Monterey fishing industry, which prospered with rail connection to San Francisco.   [72-08-54]

"THE QUEEN OF AMERICAN WATERING PLACES"

The magnificent Hotel Del Monte was constructed in less than half a year and opened its doors on June 3, 1880 to throngs of prominent and wealthy patrons from around the world. They were fetched by carriage from the hotel's own "Del Monte Station" on the new Southern Pacific line completed from the main line at Castroville. Its over 160 acres boasted exotic gardens, a lake, four heated swimming pools, a polo field, amusements and accommodations fit for royalty.

Perhaps its most unusual entertainment was the "seventeen-mile drive" through the crumbling adobes of Monterey, past the curious Chinatown to the Pacific Grove gate, and on to the "pebbled beach" on Carmel Bay. The original drive passed through the Chinese fishing settlement at Pescadero, where Jung San Choy and his family set up what may have been Monterey's first souvenir stand in 1881, selling abalone shells and other curios to the more adventurous of the grand hotel's carriage trade. The rustic log Del Monte Lodge was at the time only a stop to water or change horses on the continuing trip through Carmel to the Mission and the return trip over the Carmel hill to Monterey.

The lavish hotel was destroyed by fire in 1887, and rebuilt from its original plans. Its Lodge at Pebble Beach on Carmel Bay was lost to fire in 1917 and reopened with adjoining lodging in 1919 — the same year its golf course opened on the plateaus above Pebble Beach, a panorama which no longer included the Chinese.

The hub of wealth and social activity of the Monterey Peninsula, the lavish hotel was to have a major impact on the economics of tourism and residential elegance.
C.W.J. Johnson photo, circa 1880. [79-106-8]

The 17-Mile Drive passed first through old Monterey, as seen from the roof of the Custom House in this photo by C.W.J. Johnson, 1893. The two-story adobe Pacific Building at the right survives.   [78-36-1]

The world-famous "17-Mile Drive" circa 1910, when horse drawn carriages had been replaced by automobiles like the "Winton 6" seen in this photo taken near Pescadero Point, not far from the lodge on Carmel Bay.   [72-08-45]

A souvenir stand—one of Monterey's earliest—was set up by Jung San Choy and his family beside their house on the 17-Mile Drive, on the shoreline above what is now Stillwater Cove.   Joseph K. Oliver photo. [78-62-1]

The home and family of Jung San Choy, leader of the Chinese fishing village at Pescadero on Carmel Bay. The Chinese had fished Carmel Bay from their earlier settlement at Point Lobos since 1851.   [72-17-84]

Another portion of the Pescadero Chinese fishing village from an 1880's photograph of what is now the location of the Beach and Tennis Club of the Lodge at Pebble Beach.   Joseph K. Oliver photo. [71-18-3]

The gentlemen in the derby in this 1911 R.J. Arnold photo of an arrival at the log Lodge at Pebble Beach is photographer Dan Freeman. Auto travel greatly facilitated access to the shores of Carmel Bay from Monterey.   [82-29-11]

The graphic origin of a name: the pebbled beach on Carmel Bay. The 17-Mile Drive continued along the plateaus above the beaches nearly to Carmel before climbing the hilly return trip to the Hotel Del Monte. [72-17-70]

Early Carmel, developed by L. Frank Devendorf and Frank Powers, was a curiosity often worth a side trip from the 17-Mile Drive. By 1905 Carmel sported the chimneyed Pine Inn, as seen in this E.A. Cohen photo. [2223]

The restoration of Mission San Carlos Borromeo del Rio Carmelo began with an 1883 donation by Mrs. Leland Stanford. Lewis Josselyn captures the restoration progress and a Pierce-Arrow in this 1919 photo. [70-01]

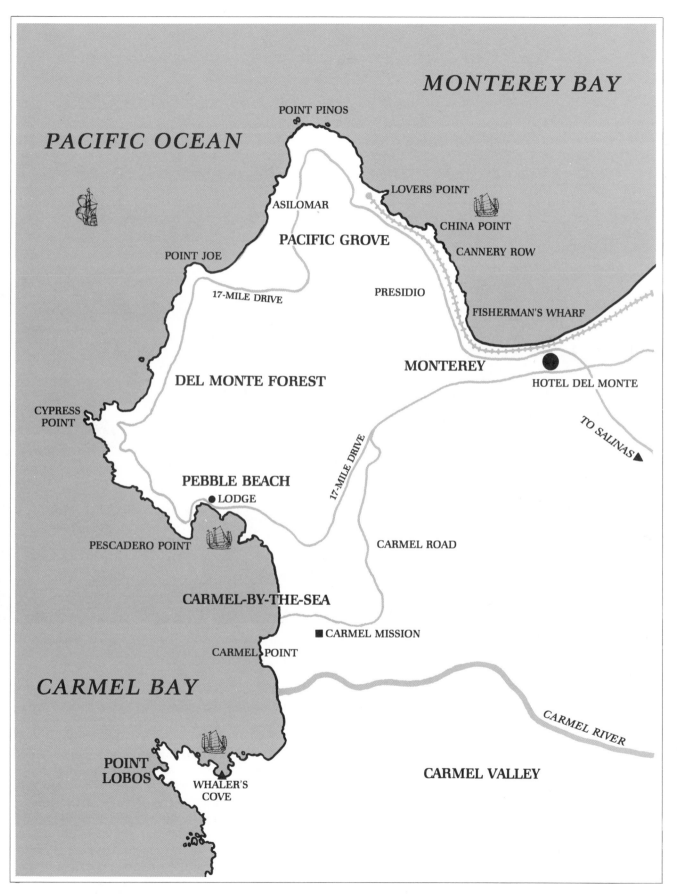

MONTEREY BAY

PACIFIC OCEAN

POINT PINOS

ASILOMAR

LOVERS POINT

PACIFIC GROVE

CHINA POINT

CANNERY ROW

POINT JOE

PRESIDIO

17-MILE DRIVE

FISHERMAN'S WHARF

MONTEREY

HOTEL DEL MONTE

DEL MONTE FOREST

TO SALINAS ▲

CYPRESS
POINT

17-MILE DRIVE

PEBBLE BEACH

● LODGE

PESCADERO POINT

CARMEL ROAD

CARMEL-BY-THE-SEA

■ CARMEL MISSION

CARMEL POINT

CARMEL BAY

CARMEL RIVER

POINT
LOBOS

WHALER'S
COVE

CARMEL VALLEY

The sheltered cove which the Chinese first settled, used briefly by the shore-whaling Portuguese, became a major Japanese

ABALONE AND THE JAPANESE

Japanese immigrants arriving in the early 1890's were predominantly farmers, but word soon spread of the area's fishing and abalone potential. One of those responding was Genno-suke Kodani, a marine biologist with extensive experience in hard hat diving technology — credentials that would establish the Monterey abalone industry. Arriving in 1896, he completed a reconnaissance of the coast for the ideal location, which he found at Point Lobos — along with its owner A.M. Allen, who quickly became his partner.

Abalone diving, employing experienced Japanese divers, was supplemented by fishing for salmon and sardines. Canning of cubed and minced abalone for export, and salmon and sardine deliveries to Monterey's developing canneries soon established a solid Japanese presence on the coast. Along with it came the prejudicial treatment and regulation so familiar to the Chinese before them.

The shoreline canneries of Monterey, however, were grateful for their diving expertise in the

abalone operation. Dan Freeman's photo shows the cannery opposite Coal Chute Point, 1905.   [73-35-2]

repair and early maintenance of the offshore anchors for the cables by which sardines were unloaded by bucket-and-pulley to the canneries. The Japanese led the way for American diving development, an indispensable asset in future canning technology. Japanese cannery labor, specializing in the cutting operation, also became a major factor in the economic life of Cannery Row.

At its height, Point Lobos diving boats numbered up to eighteen — each with a crew of four — some operating as far south as Moro Bay. For a time the flagship of this Point Lobos flotilla was the "Ocean Queen," a sizeable rumrunner's boat abandoned in hot pursuit at the cove and later bought at auction from the government during Prohibition. Prior to 1941, most of the fish processors and fish markets on Monterey's Fisherman's Wharf were Japanese owned and operated. Wartime expropriation of these businesses and internment of Monterey's Japanese American citizens during World War II ended the Japanese influence in Monterey's fishing economy.

Gennosuke Kodani (center) and crew with drying abalone on Coal Chute Point, circa 1905. Although not yet appreciated by American palates, canned minced and diced abalone was shipped to Japan as a delicacy. [72-08-175]

Carmelo Land and Coal Company's unprofitable Coal Chute Point venture did not deter the use of its location for drying abalone, as seen in this E.A. Cohen photo, circa 1905. [2276]

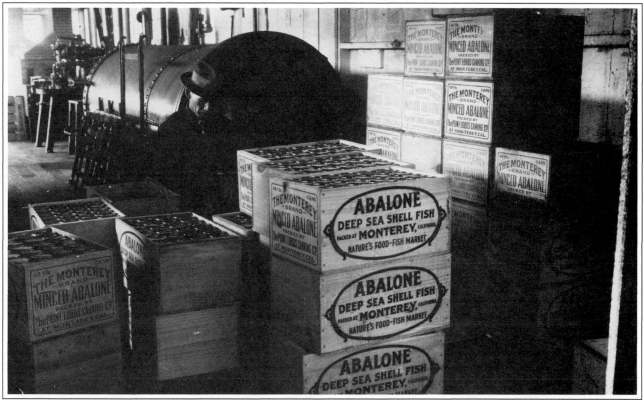

Lewis Josselyn records the interior of the Point Lobos Canning Company abalone canning operation, 1916. This early canning technology was to launch the first canning operation on old Ocean View Avenue.   [71-01-PL11]

One Japanese boat tows another dive boat from the protected cove, past the cannery at "Whaler's Cove"—a name that has stuck through two oriental occupations of Point Lobos—in this 1902 photo by an unknown photographer.   [72-08-176]

Photographer Lewis Josselyn again provides us with this amazing photograph of one of the Japanese divers, recruited by Kodani largely from the Chiba area of Tokyo Bay, for the dangerous deep harvest of abalone. [71-01-PL5]

38

The new technology of hard hat diving for abalone was to have important ramifications for the young sardine industry which was also to become dependent on diving technology. Lewis Josselyn photo, 1916. [71-01-PL6]

The rum-running Ocean Queen, which became the flagship of the Japanese abalone flotilla operating from the cove at Point Lobos. Photographer unknown, 1924. [83-46-1]

PORTUGUESE WHALING AND McABEE BEACH

Whaling in the Monterey Bay dates back to the Spanish period when New Bedford deep-water whalers anchored in the harbor to resupply for their ship-based assaults on the migrating giants. The grey and humpback varieties were so plentiful, and migrated so close to Monterey's peninsula that, in 1854, Captain John Pope Davenport organized the first "shore whaling" enterprise in Monterey. Its all-Portuguese crews were experienced whalers, many with deepwater and shore whaling experience from their native Azores Islands.

In the years following Monterey's near depopulation by the gold rush, the growth of several Portuguese-manned shore whaling companies must have provided what little excitement could be seen. Longboats were sailed and rowed from shore to meet the hapless targets of harpoon and bomb-lance. A successful strike with the "Greener's" (harpoon) gun ensured a wild ride as the longboat was dragged great distances at high speed behind the wounded whale before it tired and could be dispatched and towed back to shore.

"Try-works" on the shores below Monterey's first Whaling Station and Jack Swan's place, near the Custom House, and later at McAbee Beach on what is now Cannery Row, rendered the blubber into oil as the whales were flensed on the beaches. The stench of boiling whale blubber was another olfactory fact of life in early Monterey, as whale bones were being piled nearly the length of the beach at Monterey.

Kerosene would replace whale oil by the turn of the century as its Portuguese practitioners turned to fishing and farming. The coastal freighter "Gypsy," seen again in this 1890's flensing of a humpback at McAbee Beach, was to run aground in fog and sink at this site on September 27, 1905.

Portuguese shore-whalers flensing a humpback whale on McAbee Beach in the 1890's. Kerosene would doom such whaling operations at Monterey, vacating this once remote beach for other ventures.   C.W.J. Johnson photo. [72-17-36]

EARLY GRANDEUR

Certainly influenced by the stately splendor of the grand Hotel Del Monte — and with the added advantage of a sweeping panorama of the Monterey Bay — a magnificent estate was begun on the shores of a sandy beach on Ocean View Avenue in 1901. Son of the wealthy Lloyd Tevis, Hugh Tevis had assumed full-time management of the family investments, including property in Monterey, upon the death of his father in 1889. In 1880, his father had declared the opulent Hotel Del Monte the official family summer residence and entertained lavishly there for many years.

Hugh Tevis' first wife, Alice, died after the birth of their daughter, Alice Boalt Tevis, who was raised by her grandmother. She traveled and vacationed frequently with her father. It was on such a trip, staying at the Del Monte, that she met Cornelia Baxter, a "princess" whom she insisted her father meet.

The gorgeous eighteen-year-old debutante from a wealthy Denver family had been sent to the Hotel Del Monte to recuperate from typhoid. The romance that ensued soon resulted in their engagement in March and their marriage in April, 1901. Hugh's wedding present to his young bride, which was intended as a summer home, was to be completed that September. It was on a trip to the orient to shop for furnishings while the estate neared completion that Hugh Tevis died in Yokahama from appendicitis. Cornelia and relatives moved into the palatial estate in September, 1901, where she remained until the birth of her son, Hugh, in San Francisco the following February. The mansion would be sold.

The newly sold "Casa del las Olas" (House of the Waves) built by Hugh Tevis, passed quickly through the hands of David Jacks, to be purchased by James A. Murray in 1904. Although not a "Copper King" himself, Murray ascended into the ranks of Montana mining millionaires with a midas touch in his tough but honest financial dealings. An occasional visitor and heavy spender at the Hotel Del Monte, his wealth required a suitable residence as he eyed Monterey for his retirement with his second wife, Mary, and her son, Stuart Haldorn. His was not a full retirement to Monterey, as he kept up his financial interests while embarking into the arena of local art and history patronage.

Perhaps having been a mining man kept him

The elegant Tevis-Murray Estate, occupying a thousand feet of coastline, was inspired by the fabulous grandeur of the Hotel Del Monte. Who could have foreseen its ironic and ignominious fate?   [79-43-2]

The grand Casa de las Olas, "House of the Waves," built by Hugh Tevis as a summer house for his young bride, a Denver socialite.

from objecting to nearby storage tanks and the Associated Oil Company pier that now encroached the view from the "Murray Mansion." But how could James Murray have possibly known the future consequences of the archaic canning experiments in the Booth cannery at the harbor, or at the rudimentary sardine packing shed toward McAbee Beach that would become the Pacific Fish Company. Cannery construction along the once remote coastal road was well underway by Murray's death in 1921.

By early 1941 the estate was surrounded by the noise and smell of cannery expansion, and succumbed to that pressure. It sold to Angelo Lucido, owner of the San Carlos Cannery, who soon subdivided the property for sale to cannery and reduction plant development. The halcyon days of the Tevis-Murray estate were over; it was demolished in 1944.

Though beautiful, this property has not enjoyed good fortune. Postcard, date unknown.   [79-81-2]

THE McABEE CHINATOWN

The whalers were gone from the beach and little disturbed the tranquility of the nearby Murray estate until the fire that destroyed the major Chinese settlement at China Point in 1906. The fire triggered several important changes: it dispersed a large portion of the once thriving Chinese enclave, it ended the Chinese participation in the further development of the Monterey fishing industry, and it resulted in the successful negotiation for a new but smaller Chinatown at McAbee Beach.

McAbee, a Scotsman, had developed a leisurely seaside tent-cottage and boat rental business just prior to the turn of the century. Summer Sundays were busy with bathers and picnickers in what was to be the last of this beach's recreational enterprises. The nearly vacant beach would become Chinese, over the strenuous objections of Murray and other local dignitaries, as China Point's refugees obtained leases from the Scot.

By 1910 the industrious "newcomers" had erected a somewhat more conventional-appearing settlement above the beach, facing Ocean View Avenue. Included were the Joss House, which had escaped the fire, and the Monterey Fishing and Canning Company, engaged almost entirely in reducing fish heads and offal from Booth and Pacific Fish Co. to fertilizer — Monterey's first major "reduction" plant. Now inside the Monterey city limits, the Chinese were prohibited from drying squid at McAbee's and moved that operation to the highway toward Salinas, outside city jurisdiction. As more Chinese moved out of fishing, an Oriental quarter grew up at Franklin and Washington Streets in downtown Monterey, containing both Chinese and Japanese. The once proud Ocean View Hotel was built in 1927 above the vacated beach by Chinese investors Wu and Sam.

The McAbee Chinatown circa 1911 with its reduction plant (with smokestack), and on the far right, the Joss House—saved by its distance from the fire at China Point—in its second location. J.K. Oliver photo. [73-12-3]

44

The stylish Ocean View Hotel, built on the McAbee Chinatown site by investors Wu and Sam, seen in this photo circa 1934, taken by an unidentified photographer.   Photo Courtesy James Wu. [86-51-01]

PACIFIC GROVE AT PLAY

The Chinese and their squid drying had been vanquished by fire; their move to New Monterey's McAbee Beach had ended the only other nearby boating and seaside recreation. With a Japanese Tea Garden and other tourist and entertainment establishments completed, Lovers of Jesus Point in Pacific Grove took on new life.

Among its newly famous attractions was a glass bottomed boat concession, a bath house, a heated salt-water swimming pool, auditorium and photography studio. An even earlier structure — the Hopkins Seaside Laboratory — had opened on the point in 1892, a gift of Timothy Hopkins and the Pacific Improvement Company, the first such research facility to study the marine life on the west coast.

After the fire at China Point, the dilemma as to what to do with the land — earlier marked for development of expensive residential homesites — was resolved. The Pacific Improvement Company donated the land to the University of California for use as a location for a marine research and laboratory station. By 1917 the Hopkins Seaside Laboratory had reopened as the Hopkins Marine Station, relocated from Lovers of Jesus Point to China Point, and now affiliated with Stanford University.

Unfortunately, the curriculum did not deal with either salmon ... or the *sardine*.

Autumn of 1907 at Lovers of Jesus Point, Pacific Grove. The swan-necked glass bottomed boats had been built by Russell Sprague in 1886. A "lookout" building and Japanese Tea House dominate the point.   [72-08-91]

Hopkins Seaside Laboratory, in this 1890's photo, was another occupant of Lovers of Jesus Point until moved to China Point in 1917 as Hopkins Marine Station of Stanford University. [72-08-80]

IT ALL STARTED WITH SALMON

Monterey's early commercial fishermen were by stock a hardy and independent group, in many ways reflecting the state of the "industry" of the times. The Chinese were doing a brisk business to their San Francisco and overseas markets. The Genovese, or mainland Italians, were doing a profitable business in "fresh" fish of many varieties. The Spanish-speaking "Californios" could boast the first salmon caught (unintentionally) trolling: a fifty-three pounder which induced a concerted effort at hook-and-line attempts to add this magnificent species to the Monterey inventory. Of all the market varieties being fished in Monterey, none was to be more important to the turn-of-the-century bay area economy than salmon.

Commission agents had ventured to Monterey since the early 1890's to buy salmon for packing plants at San Francisco and the Sacramento River. One such visitor was Frank E. Booth, president of the Sacramento River Packer's Association, who by 1896 concluded that Monterey's salmon supply warranted a local cannery. In 1896, Booth built but shortly closed an experimental salmon canning shed adjacent to the Pacific Coast Steamship Company pier as local fishermen accepted higher bids from San Francisco agents. Their greed was rewarded by lower prices again after Booth's withdrawal.

Booth tried again in 1901, but was no longer the only packer at Monterey. San Franciscan H.R. Robbins had constructed a small wharf, complete with a smoke house and warehouse, also adjacent to the steamship pier. Both operated successfully, but with much difficulty in 1902 before Booth's canning operation was destroyed by fire. Robbin's operation faltered badly and could not take advantage of Booth's ill fortune. His experiments in reduction of scraps and salmon waste, however, proved an interesting and somewhat lucrative sideline — but unable to save him. Booth returned in 1903, buying out the entire Robbins cannery.

This early postcard clearly explains the initial interests in Monterey as a fishing town. It was salmon like this that brought the fish buyers to Monterey, later to experiment in sardine canning.   [86-12-4]

It was *salmon* that put Monterey on the commercial map at the turn of the century and another postcard clearly reflects the bounty of its beautiful bay waters, with 7000 salmon caught in a single day.   [78-62-1]

Frank E. Booth, "Father of the Monterey Sardine Industry"—an early fish buyer for his Sacramento River cannery—was to establish a salmon and then sardine canning operation in Monterey.

[78-47-1]

THE UNSUNG ORIGIN

The entry of Booth's "Monterey Packing Company" consolidation of 1903 into the fish packing business was preceded a year by a rudimentary canning-shed operation begun on the rocky New Monterey coastline. Harry Malpas, with canning experience from the Point Lobos Canning Company and backed by Japanese investment, opened the first canning operation on Ocean View Avenue — destined to become Cannery Row. His small-scale "Monterey Fishing and Canning Company" opened in March, 1902, and struggled with the same fishermen's infidelities and erratic supplies of fish as did Booth and Robbins, but with far fewer reserves.

Booth's general manager since 1902 was replaced by the young Norwegian canning specialist, Knut Hovden, in 1905. James A. Madison, who had joined a San Francisco canning company returned in 1907 and with Joseph Nichols negotiated the purchase of the financially troubled Malpas packing business. Another of the investors was Bernard Senderman of Pittsburg. On February 14, 1908, "Pacific Fish Company" was born — the first major cannery on Ocean View Avenue.

"Cannery" requires some explanation and in many ways the Pacific Fish Company is a typical early profile. The delivery of fish was accomplished at a pier, constructed as far out over the rocky shoreline as possible. Fish were cut by hand to remove heads, tails and offal. They were then split and spread to drain and dry on wooden "flakes," or slats. Large flat metal baskets of "flaked" fish were then drawn through long troughs of boiling peanut oil, drained again, packed into cans and *hand soldered* closed. Labeling and boxing for warehousing and shipment completed the process. This process, with some variation, was common to all the early Monterey canneries. A gifted man was to change all that.

The forerunner of Pacific Fish Co., backed by Japanese investment and experience from the Point Lobos cannery, was established a year before F.E. Booth began major sardine canning at the harbor in 1903. [83-41-1]

This 1911 photo of the Pacific Fish Co. crew shows the splitting and drying of sardines prior to boiling in oil and canning, in a rudimentary process that included hand-soldering the cans closed.   [81-14-1]

Pacific Fish Co. was incorporated in 1908, replacing the early Monterey Fishing and Canning Company. It became the first "major" canning operation on the rocky New Monterey coastline, to become Cannery Row.   [83-13-1]

A view from Wave Street shows Hopkins Marine Station, Monterey Boatworks—on the former Chinatown site—and the cannery

THE PRINCE AND SOON KING

In 1905 the most important man in Monterey's sardine saga took a position with Booth's awkward and poorly mechanized canning operation at the harbor. The young Knut Hovden, a talented graduate of the Norwegian Fisheries College, had immigrated from the North Sea canning industry due to a serious respiratory problem. He brought with him both experience in an advanced canning technology and a gift of inventive genius. The archaic canning procedures he found in Monterey gave him a challenge and opportunity to apply both.

A self emptying "purse-bottom brailing net" was one of his first applied solutions to the ardu-

ous unloading of sardines from the lighters (barges) in which they were delivered to the cannery. The canning itself was to benefit enormously from his invention of a mechanical sealer-solderer, permitting an astonishing increase in production capacity. His almost immediate impact on the capacity of Booth's processing was unmatched, however, by a corresponding improvement in the increased capture and delivery of sardines. Both local fishermen and their clumsy gill nets were unsuitable to the expansion of production capacity Hovden had made possible.

The impasse was to be broken by another

of Knut Hovden, circa 1918. Note the horses still in use at Great Western Sardine Co.

man of vision and "appropriate technology," a respected Sicilian fisherman from Booth's Sacramento River operation. Pietro Ferrante represented both the tough Sicilian work ethic and the intelligence to apply a familiar technique utilized by his Mediterranean ancestors — the "lampara" net.

Unlike the clumsy and inefficient gill net, which was dragged into a school of sardines which were caught in it by their gills — requiring removal by hand after capture — the "lightning" net in the 1907 experiments at Monterey encircled the sardines and was then quickly closed at its ends to entrap its catch.

Booth's new canning capacity would now soon be matched by a substantial improvement in the delivery of sardines — by Sicilians who knew how to conduct the lampara technique. So would begin the Sicilian mastery of the Monterey sardine fishing industry.

Hovden was soon happily seeking ways to keep canning capacity up with the rapidly burgeoning delivery rate, a situation challenging his inventiveness and an opportunity he eagerly pursued. His processing prowess was to become legend and the opportunity to employ his innovations in a canning facility of his own was a certain expectation as he assumed a larger and larger role in the Booth operation. It is appropriate that Frank

One of a series of industrial photographs taken in the early 1920's provides a look at the make-up of the K. Hovden Company crew

Booth should be called the "Father of the sardine industry," but the young Hovden would soon be "King."

By 1915 it had become evident to Hovden that his once grateful and cooperative employer, Frank Booth, was stubbornly resisting changes and improvements he sought in the further development of his processing techniques. Hovden's interest in the potentially lucrative reduction and sardine by-product business may have proven the last straw. Without Booth's cooperation, he ventured into a small reduction development which proved a profitable sideline to the existing canning process.

Max N. Schaefer, a vigorous and innovative businessman, was further convinced that reduction could be a *major* part of the industry and developed full-scale reduction as a separate industrial enterprise. His plant in San Francisco's San Pablo Bay provided the model for his "Monterey Fish Products Company," which opened in 1915 on Cannery Row.

Hovden submitted his resignation in November, 1915, and with the support of local financier and real estate man T.A. Work, opened the "Hovden Cannery" at the north end of Ocean View Avenue on July 7, 1916. Once Prince, the King had now arrived.

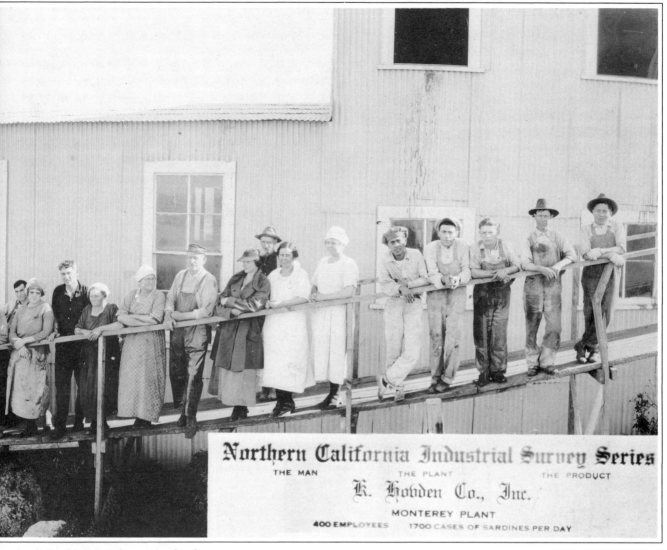

Northern California Industrial Survey Series

THE MAN   THE PLANT   THE PRODUCT

K. Hovden Co., Inc.

MONTEREY PLANT

400 EMPLOYEES   1700 CASES OF SARDINES PER DAY

in the early years of cannery development.   [86-52-1]

THE STARTING GUN

Assuming a position at the head of the pack he would never relinquish, Hovden's entry into the sardine packing industry could hardly have come at a better time. The "Great War" was to shut down the North Sea fishery, leaving Monterey's inexpensive, high-protein sardine pack in extremely high demand as a wartime ration.

By war's end, Booth, Pacific Fish, and Hovden canneries would be joined by:

California Fisheries Company, a Japanese export firm;

Bayside Cannery near Hovden's;

Monterey Canning Company, owned by George Harper and A.M. Allen of Point Lobos abalone canning;

San Xavier Canning Co. near the Murray estate;

What was to become Carmel Canning Company, for Bernard Senderman, early partner in Pacific Fish Company;

E.B. Gross Cannery, near the Murray Estate;

And a Brick reduction plant on Foam Street for the late entry of Frank Booth to the by-products business, joining Max Schaefer's Monterey Fish Products Co. in major reduction processing.

Cannery Row's wartime production would grow from 75,000 cases in 1915 to 1,400,000 cases in 1918; the price per case rose from $2.14 to $7.50 through that same period. The apparent result of World War I on Cannery Row was to provide the investment incentive to develop and mechanize the canning industry at Monterey. It was also an important step in helping overcome resistance in world markets to the large Pacific cousin of the widely accepted Atlantic Sardine. In the United States a domestic market had hardly existed. This unprecedented wartime bonanza was, of course, too good to last; recession set in as the guns cooled.

Perhaps quaint by current standards, the rugged, highly competitive sardine canning business resulted in canneries and warehouses of strictly functional design, although some bore barn-like advertising of the day.   [83-41-2]

A LOOK AROUND

A glimpse down Cannery Row in the aftermath of the war would show a boomtown of corrugated canneries perched over a rocky coastline, unloading sardines from offshore by cable and bucket — 500 pounds at a time. Although canning had been significantly mechanized, labor continued a major factor in production.

In an age before telephones in the working class home, the cannery workers were called to work by cannery whistle; each cannery had a distinct pitch and pattern. Working hours were dictated by the arrival and size of each day's catch. Work itself was generally cold, wet and smelly, in drafty plank and tin canneries where the din of steam, cascading cans and the roar of equipment often drowned out an orchestra of international languages spoken in the primarily Chinese and Japanese cutting rooms and sheds — the Spanish, Portuguese, Sicilian, Mexican and English of the canning lines — and the shouts, grunts and curses of the warehousing crews.

Monterey's initial displeasure with the odors from Robbin's early salmon reduction experiments around 1902 were merely memories. But the smell of reduction would become, in the decade of the twenties, a problem of major proportion. The Chinese at McAbee had led the Row into reduction and its wrenching smell, augmented by Hovden's similar interests and the success of Max Schaefer's leadership in the processing technique. Even the stubborn Frank Booth had succumbed to its profits and utility. The net effect was a well-earned reputation best summed up by a saying of the times: "Carmel by the Sea, Pacific Grove by God ... and Monterey by the smell!" But in these uncertain times it was also "The smell of prosperity." The industry and its workforce tolerated it; the City of Monterey objected to it; the Hotel Del Monte's Samuel F.B. Morse was infuriated by it, and yet because the industry's continued survival — at least as it was structured — depended on it, the death-like stench should have been seen as a warning of something inherently wrong about its necessity.

RETHINKING REDUCTION

The post-war era posed problems old and new. Without wartime demand, and with the resumption of the Atlantic sardine fishery, foreign markets resumed their nearly non-existent status, as did the domestic market. Unfavorable tariffs simply compounded perhaps the biggest problem: canner's speculation had resulted in warehouses full of sardines. As canneries sold, closed or went bankrupt, a "bailout" was needed.

Reduction and its huge profits on minimal investment and labor costs could no longer be ignored. The industry entered the 1920's with an ever-increasing pressure for legislation to permit larger scale reduction and by-product use of the catch. Warnings by the state's Department of Fish and Game specialists were pitted against industry survival and the jobs at stake. It was either fish or jobs — reduction profits would subsidize the depressed canning industry. The decade of the twenties was to establish the irreversible direction of the industry to profit at the uncertain expense of the fishery. Besides, as Hovden would state, "The sardine supply could not be exterminated" — at a time when certain proof could not be produced to the contrary.

The investment effect of The Great War saw canneries constructed high over the rocky shores of Ocean View Avenue, off-loading sardines by bucket-and-cable in the 1920's to avoid dangerous underwater rocks and reefs. [73-20-14]

Sardines were delivered to canneries by barges called "lighters" after a night of fishing, unloaded into buckets—500 pounds at a time—up the cables to Ocean View Avenue canneries. [73-20-12]

The bucket hoists at the top of the canneries received the off-loaded sardines for measurement and weighing. The canning process then began in cutting sheds and rooms, also usually in the upper levels of the canneries. [73-20-13]

Ocean View Avenue canning was truly an international pursuit, from its markets to its workforce. The crew of the Bayside Cannery is typical of the multi-nationality labor force in Monterey's canning industry. [78-01-13]

ACTS OF GOD AND TRIALS BY FIRE

The powerful Pacific was to shake any complacency from its Monterey mariners with its periodic ravaging of the unprotected fleet; no breakwater would be constructed until the early thirties. The worst such storm destroyed 93 lampara boats on the Monterey Beach on Thanksgiving, 1919 — an especially heavy blow given the post-war recession in the fishing and canning industry. It would take another "natural" disaster to provide the protection the harbor needed.

The nearby petroleum storage tanks which Murray had ignored when purchasing the Tevis estate were struck by lightning on September 14, 1924. The fire lasted for days before exploding into a river of flaming oil running into the sea. In its path were the canneries of California Fisheries and E.B. Gross — and the Murray estate. The canneries were destroyed and the mansion only narrowly escaped the same fate. The Associated Oil Company Pier — which dispensed petroleum to its ocean freighter traffic — was destroyed completely as the oil, blazing on the bay, drifted perilously toward Fisherman's Wharf ... until the tide changed!

Only two weeks later, on the night of September 28, the luxurious Hotel Del Monte burned to the ground for the second time. It would reopen, redesigned, the following May.

Fire would also call on Knut Hovden ... twice. The first major fire on August 12, 1921 destroyed the cannery in a fire that lasted two days, fed by vats of sardine oil. His reconstruction included a larger and more modern plant. The second fire occurred October 5, 1924, guting the reduction plant in a $20,000 inferno. But the King of Cannery Row each time rebuilt, although at great difficulty in the recession-plagued early twenties.

Fisherman's Wharf and Booth were not to escape the call of fate. By the first of March, 1923, canneries had loaded the wharf with twenty thousand cases of sardines for shipment on the freighter "San Antonio." Without a breakwater yet to shield the harbor from unpredictable swells, the "San Antonio" lurched against the Wharf, damaging it and dumping 8,000 cases of still-to-be-loaded sardines into the bay.

Frank Booth was to be the victim of a similar fate on February 2, 1927, when 4,000 cases fell through the floors of his warehouse into the bay. The twenties had, indeed, "roared" in Monterey.

The devastating Thanksgiving Day storm of 1919 wrecked nearly the entire Monterey lampara fishing fleet, at an already poor time in the recession plagued industry's post-war recovery.   Lewis Josselyn photo. [71-01-311]

Photographer Charles Tuttle provides this view of the oil tank fire in its early stages. Neither the Monterey Fire Department nor the military was equipped to combat this type of conflagration. [82-29-32]

After burning several days the tanks finally exploded in a flaming river of oil to the sea, destroying the canneries of E.B. Gross and California Fisheries Co. and threatening the Murray mansion. Dan Freeman photo. [85-11-10]

The oil continued to burn on the surface of Monterey Bay as Fisherman's Wharf and the Booth cannery were in its path until,

fatefully, wind and tide changed to save them. This drama is recorded by Dan Freeman.   [82-29-29]

Cannery baron E.B. Gross watches on as Cecil Gretter opens the cannery safe amid the ashes of his cannery. Gross would rebuild and become one of the major figures in Monterey's sardine industry.

Freeman photo. [85-11-01]

METAMORPHOSIS

It was as if the whole of Monterey was caught up in a sudden, accelerated transformation. The sleepy, isolated pueblo of Spanish Monterey was suddenly all but gone — except for the few adobes and other early Monterey architecture saved from demolition in the awakening of a new civic consciousness. A momentum established in the twenties would carry Monterey into the decade of the thirties, including its Depression, propelled by sardines!

Lingering memories of a Chinatown, and even whaling along these shores, were quickly fading into the realities of boatyards, choruses of cannery whistles, and the steady growth of a fishing and canning industry upon which Monterey would become too dependent. Where had the little town gone? The answer lay in *sardines:* a town and nearly its entire economy was becoming tied up in, serving or prospering in the commerce of one of the world's greatest natural resources, *Sardinops caerulea.*

As long as the supply of sardines held out — and with little expression of concern except the biennial Department of Fish & Game reports of the imminent depletion that must be coming, but could not be proven — invention and investment had become partners with work and pay. It was the convergence of technical advances and commercial opportunity that would doom the 12-inch fish that greased the gears of prosperity in a decade that first had to rise from the greatest depression in our nation's experience.

Alvarado Street, 1920, with its street-car tracks and establishments, including the Poppy—used in John Steinbeck's *Sweet Thursday*—and the Bay State Cafe of Mr. Wu (Ocean View Hotel). R.J. Arnold photo. [78-36-3]

Memories of boatbuilding and bootlegging, and especially one foggy 1927 rum-runners vs. police shootout at the old boatyard,

The Pacific Fleet called on Monterey August 31, 1919, its harbor still without Wharf #2 and the protective breakwater that would

were fading in Monterey's growth into real cityhood.
A.C. Heidrick photo, 1918. [82-40-1]

be eventually constructed in 1932-34. A.C. Heidrick records the last such naval vista.
[79-104-3]

THE MEN, THE BOATS

Pietro Ferrante, Orazio Enea, Salvatore Russo, Constantine Balbo, Marco Lucido and Salvatore Lucido — men fated to come to Monterey in 1907 from Black Diamond (now Pittsburg) on the Sacramento River — had set out in the "Crescent" and "Queen Esther" on a Monterey experiment with a Mediterranean net for a fish other men still had to learn to can. Their success saw the romantic felucca's that once dotted the bay with their lanteen sails, yield to "Monterey Clippers" towing lighters of fish back to the harbor or anchoring off Cannery Row to unload by bucket-and-cable.

The success of the lampara boat and its role in cannery supply seemed a near perfect match for the predominantly Sicilian immigrants that first manned, and then owned them. Their cost and that of the net was within the reach of many of the fishing families being established on the hill behind the harbor. Several men and a great deal of hard work could produce a good, if frugal livelihood — even ownership of a good and lucky boat. But they had set in motion forces that would soon make the ever improving technology the master, not the servant, of the men who followed its call to the sea.

The insatiable appetites of Monterey's canneries and reduction plants now required a far more complex organization of the means of supply. Establishing the season price between canners and fishermen grew more complicated as the number of boats and owners multiplied into the 1920's. An effective strike for a price increase by the combined boatowners and fishermen in the 1926 season was to bring far-reaching consequences, again at the hands of technology. Hovden threatened to break the strike by bringing boats up from San Pedro, which as a tuna port brought into the sardine business by World War I, was far ahead of Monterey in vessel development.

On July 19, 1926 the purse seiners "Admiral" and "Mariposa" cruised into Monterey Bay. The vessels were larger and swifter than anything Monterey's lampara fleet could have imagined. Their size, at over fifty feet in length, incorporated a protected wheel-house and cabin, large diesel engines, power winches for the huge purse seine, a revolving turntable aft on which the net was stacked for deployment and a *hold* capacity of thirty-five tons! It meant no more lighters to be towed, a range that opened up new fishing grounds, and an enormous net that closed at the bottom to securely entrap far greater amounts of

sardines at a time than a canner's dream. A month later the strike was settled in a compromise, but Monterey had again been changed forever: the means by which the unconscious depletion of the sardine could be accomplished had arrived.

The introduction of the purse seiner brought with it a wave of controversy in the boatowners and fishermen's ranks. A show-down of old friends led "Pete" Ferrante into retirement as Orazio Enea's demands for a "closed shop" organization of boatowners and fishermen heated up a tangled series of organizational attempts dating back to 1914. The reconciliation also had an interesting side effect. Won Yee, the squid baron of Monterey, had used the internal division of boatowner groups for years to form a squid marketing monopoly in which the Sicilian rivalries insured the depressed price of squid, much to Yee's stoic benefit. Sicilian lampara technology, which had eliminated the Chinese from their own squid fishing industry, had made unwitting restitution.

The cost of entry into this new age of big boats and huge nets was, of course, astronomical by Monterey standards. A "half-ring" net, resembling the purse seine, was installed on most of the lampara boats as a stop-gap measure. Requiring little modification to the boats, it could capture nearly the same tonnage as the early purse seine — but still required the use of the accompanying lighter in which to put the catch. The purse seiner age had arrived amid resentment and controversy in the lampara entrenched industry at Monterey.

In an ironic twist, the "Admiral" sank in January 1928, fortunately without loss of life, attempting to haul in an oversize catch. The first small Monterey-built purse seiner, the "Santa Lucia," joined the fleet the following season under contract to the E.B. Gross Cannery. Legislation in 1929 also established the Monterey sardine season between August 1 and February 15. Within the next few seasons the replacement of the lampara by half-rings was followed by new and even larger purse seines and seiners, setting the stage for an awesome new fishing capability centered around the new wolves of the sea.

Through the thirties the expansion of the Monterey sardine fleet and matching canning capacity would record annual tonnage landed at Monterey in excess of 200,000 *tons* per season in 1934-35, 1936-37, and 1939-40. The decade of the thirties was to be fraught with controversy and

(continued on page 73)

The immigrating Italians contested Chinese use of the Bay in feluccas, the sailboat design familiar from their Mediterranean experience. This photo also shows the early Pacific Steamship Company pier and steamer. [83-30-1]

The Thad is typical of early lampara boats, too small to carry crew, net and fish—requiring the towing of a lighter in which to put the catch for transport back to bucket lines or Booth's pier. F.C. Swain photo. [81-39-2]

Booth Cannery's harbor location afforded direct, dockside off-loading of lighters. This photo shows the "brailing" of sardines from the "S. Oyama" at the Booth Cannery for processing.   [74-20-1]

Nino Di Maggio's "Caterina," seen at Booth's with lighters, is typical of the "Monterey Clipper" design utilized by the Sicilian lampara fishermen of the 1920's: its unique bow design deflected waves. [74-20-10]

The lampara nets, which encircled its catch, were spread for repair behind Booth's Cannery, as well as many other Monterey locations where these increasingly large nets could be maintained. Lewis Josselyn photo, 1929. [71-01-173]

Skipper John Gradis brought the "Admiral" up from San Pedro in 1926—the first such "Purse-seiner," named for the huge net it operated which could be closed at the bottom. A revolution had arrived.   [74-20-33]

Early purse-seiners replaced lampara boats as the decade of the thirties arrived, in a grudging switch to a technology as disgruntling as it was expensive—but effective beyond any question.　A.C. Heidrick photo. [73-06-42]

confrontation, almost entirely involved in the resolution of the quantities of fish the industry was to take, and what was then to be done with them. The agonizingly slow recovery from the Depression made reasoning even more difficult as the industry argued that its very survival rested on increased limits for reduction of whole fish.

Open reduction at sea by freighters converted to floating reduction plants resisted effective controls by operating beyond territorial limits until stopped by legislation in 1938. Deliveries to these "floaters" were made directly from purse seiners, whose nets were typically over a quarter of a mile long and extended to a depth of ten stories! Only time would reveal the awesome efficiency of this newest technology.

A decade of purse-seining filled Monterey harbor with the swift and efficient wolves of the sea, in a period of depression softened by the general success of Monterey's sardine industry. This panorama of Monterey's fleet includes Wharf #2 and the Booth Cannery at the right. In the foreground is the "Western Flyer," skippered by Captain Tony Berry to Baja California with John Steinbeck and Ed "Doc" Ricketts in the Spring of 1940—a year before this photo—from which came the co-authored book, *Sea of*

Cortez. The narrative portion of that work is available as *The Log from the Sea of Cortez*, carrying John Steinbeck's sole authorship, although it too is also a collaboration. Its preface, "About Ed Ricketts," is an important statement by John Steinbeck after the death of Ed Ricketts in 1948. A.C. Hiedrick photo, 1941. Courtesy Bud Hellam. [86-17-1]

Monterey's sardine fleet must have seemed strangely idle, riding at anchor in the harbor—even in season. The curious explanation is that most of Monterey's sardines were caught *at night*.   George Seideneck photo. [72-12-36]

Monterey's sardine season, August to mid-February, often involved over one hundred purse-seiners. The spectacle of such a fleet is now only a memory, but preserved in this Rey Ruppel photo of the late 1930's.   [74-08-2]

The week of the full moon each month of the season, when sardines could not be located by their nightfeeding luminescence, was spent on maintenance of the huge purse-seines, beginning onboard. Seideneck photo. [72-12-76]

The whole crew was involved in mending and preparing the huge cotton nets for the tanning tanks. Tan bark for the tank's solution came from Partington Ridge oaks on the Big Sur coatline. Fred Harbick photo. [73-06-15]

Tanning the cotton net prevented mildew and purged it of fish oils and acids in an era that could not foresee the nylon filament nets that have replaced them. Maintenance was *mandatory*.

Rey Ruppel photo. [74-08-1]

MISCONCEPTION AND TECHNIQUE

Perhaps the two most frequently misunderstood factors in the saga of Monterey sardine history concern the fish themselves and the technique of their capture. The first misconception concerns the *size* of the Monterey sardine — or pilchard — which routinely reached eleven or more inches in length. This is obviously not its finger-sized Atlantic cousin still so popular, and in commercial supply by a number of nations still in the trade. The large size of the Monterey sardine, and the weakness of a dependable domestic market made it a difficult food commodity to promote: American acceptance of canned fish of this type remained traditionally low except during wartime ration demands. Peacetime overseas markets met stiff and systematically subsidized competition by Russian, Japanese, South American and North Sea industries.

The second, and perhaps even more interesting misconception involves the fishing technique: it was conducted almost exclusively *at night*. Finding vast schools of sardines required far more than fisherman's luck: the experience of the skipper was of the utmost importance. The trained eye and experience of a seasoned skipper and crew could spot the "green flash" of phosphorescence on the dark waters of moonless nights caused by the turbulence of millions of schooling fish. Real skill could distinguish between sardines and a time and effort wasting catch of anchovy or horse mackerel.

"Making a set" with a net being deployed off a moving boat on the open sea in nearly total darkness (lights drew company and competition) required courage, skill and a level of teamwork difficult for the uninitiated to envision. Although often referred to as "Italians," the men whose labor and skill dominated the Monterey fishing industry came from the coastal cities near Palermo, Sicily. Any Sicilian will be happy to explain the difference.

The set began by dropping the skiff off the back of the seiner, to which was attached one end of the net. The crewman in the skiff deployed a sea anchor, a parachute-like device that when submerged acted like a brake, allowing the purse seiner to pull away on its arc through the portion of the school of sardines selected by the skipper. Remember the "Admiral": take as much as you can, but take *too much* and its all over. The Seiner completed its encirclement of the catch to connect its end of the net to the skiff. A cable running through rings at the bottom of the lead-weighted net was drawn in by winch to purse the net below the fish.

The boom and tackle lifted the net to the turntable as the power-winch drew in the pursed net until the last section of the net, the bag, drew alongside the purse seiner. It was only then that the skipper and crew could inspect and measure the catch, often several hundred tons, to ensure that it met minimum length specification for acceptance by Fish & Game inspectors at the canneries. This brings us to another major factor in the sardine supply: a catch of sardines too small to be landed at Monterey was dumped at sea — usually killing nearly all the sardines taken in the set. This kind of loss at sea — *before* the excesses in reduction of delivered fish — is inestimable.

A large dip-net, resembling a horn of plenty when tipped and emptied into the seiner's hold, transferred fish from the bag to boat. If the bag contained more sardines than the capacity of the seiner's hold, it was common to pour the excess fish onto the walkways and deck, which was referred to as a deck load. For exceptionally large catches, sharing the extra fish unable to be carried was common among friendly boats.

In the early thirties the cable-and-bucket method of off-loading fish to the canneries of the Row was replaced by a system of floating wooden pens, or "hoppers," anchored safely out from Cannery Row's treacherous reefs. The hoppers were connected to the canneries by large pipe-like underwater hoses, employing massive pumps to literally suck the sardines ashore for processing. This major innovation solved the tremendous problem of quickly unloading large quantities of sardines from the increasing size and number of purse-seiners entering the fleet.

0   2   4   6

INCHES

Photo by J. M. Hawthorne, Los Angeies.

FIG. 25.

CALIFORNIA SARDINE

Sardina cærulea[3]

Relationship: A true sardine, belonging to the herring family (Clupeidae), in which are also classed the herring and the shad.

Distinguishing Characters: The single, short dorsal fin near the middle of the back; the absence of scales on the head; the absence of a lateral line; the mouth opening at the tip of the head, neither jaw projecting; the gill cover having low raised ridges running obliquely downward; the breast and belly not being drawn to a sharp, saw-toothed edge, although the scales on the breast and belly have spines which can be felt when the finger is moved toward the head. **Color:** Dark green above with many small dark spots, shading into bright silvery on the sides and below; the green color having opalescent reflections, the silvery part iridescent; a series of round black spots of varying degrees of distinctness often extends backward under the scales. Attains a length of about 14 inches.

Distribution: From British Columbia southward into the Gulf of California, with largest California landings being made at Monterey, Los Angeles, San Francisco and San Diego. Occurs in schools or "shoals."

Fishing Season: Caught throughout the year with certain legal restrictions for different districts, with maximum landings in the fall and winter months.

Importance: The largest fishery in the State. Mostly canned; rather small amounts appear in the fresh fish markets and some are smoked, salted and pickled. Extensively used as bait, the young for live bait fishing.

Fishing Gear: Purse seines, and lampara or round haul nets.

---

[3] Hubbs (Calif. Acad. Sci. Proc., vol. 18, no. 11, p. 261–265, 1929) has indicated a new genus (*Sardinops*) for this fish, but for the purposes of this bulletin, the older, more familiar form is used.

Detail from the Bureau of Commercial Fisheries, Fish Bulletin No. 28: *Handbook of Common Commercial and Game Fishes of California*, by Lionel A. Walford, 1931.

The "skiff" that was to anchor one end of the huge net was also used to transport the assembled crew to its waiting purse-seiner to begin a night's search and "set" for the silver sardine.   Fred Harbick photo. [73-06-23]

"Mola!" ("Let her go!") signalled by the skipper would begin the set by launching the skiff off the back of the purse-seiner, attached to one end of the huge net. This often occurred in total darkness.   [73-40-1]

Hauling in the net was now accomplished by power winch and boom, but stacking the net on the turntable in near darkness took enormous work and skilled experience. George Robinson photo in the late 1940's.   [81-21-14]

Skill and good fortune often paid off in several hundred tons of sardines in a good set, often shared with other boats. Average purse-seiner capacity was 150-170 tons before a deck load.   [77-19-4]

The catch was transferred from the purse-seine to the hold on the seiner by a huge dip-net, often referred to as "the horn of plenty". This photo shows a Japanese crew filling its seiner's hold. [77-09-8]

The dip net on Skipper Tom Cardinalli's "City of Monterey" is a classic example of what was often referred to as "the horn of plenty," and another classic reminder of the size of the Monterey sardine.   George Robinson photo. [81-21-18]

John Steinbeck aptly described purse-seiners like Skipper John Russo's "Star of Monterey" as waddling into the Bay to offload at the cannery hoppers. Riding this low in the water meant a good catch and payday.   [80-45-3]

In the case of an exceptionally large catch that could not be contained in the hold, it was common to pour the excess sardines on the walkways in a "deck load," as on Pete Cardinale's "Geraldine-Ann." [80-57-1]

Early mornings found the fleet at the hoppers, disgorging their night's catch into the wooden pens connected by means of an underwater pipeline to the canneries for processing.   William Morgan photo from the forties. [80-45-8]

Brailing the purse-seiner's catch into the hoppers was the final step in the fishing process which saw an average of nearly a billion sardines per season delivered to the insatiable appetites of the canneries at Monterey.   [79-111-3]

CHANGING FORTUNES

The end of World War I, and its ensuing recession, saw a scramble for survival by the sardine factories along Cannery Row. The addition of new canneries contributed to the constantly changing face of the street as well.

Frank Raiter's San Xavier cannery opened at the north end of the Murray estate in 1917; Bernard Senderman, former partner in Pacific Fish Company, preferred retirement to further risk at his newly completed cannery, selling to local investors who opened it as Carmel Canning Company in January, 1920; Harry Irving's Sea Pride bought out the Great Western Sardine Company, next to Hovden's in 1925; Pacific Fish Company sold to California Packing Corporation in March, 1926; the American Can Company began construction on a huge can making plant across the Pacific Grove line in July, 1926; opened by Angelo Lucido in 1927, the San Carlos Cannery was owned by boat owners and fishermen; Bayside Fish and Flour became Cypress Canning Company briefly in 1927 before becoming Ed David's Del Mar Canning Company; Old Custom House Packing Corporation was formed in April, 1929.

What they all had in common was the processing of fish, and without great variation their geometry and layout were uncannily similar: the off-loading, weighing, cutting, packing, and cooking of the sardines were conducted on the ocean side of the street. Straddling Ocean View Avenue to connect production to the cannery's warehouses were the crossovers — or overpasses — by which canned sardines were transported across the street for storage, labeling and shipment from the Southern Pacific tracks at their back doors.

Each of the steps in processing was also roughly the same; the efficiency of the process often determined its fate.

The huge San Carlos Cannery, nearest to the breakwater, was owned by boat owners and fishermen. It was a powerful force in the Monterey industry, run by a former boat owner and fisherman, Angelo Lucido.   A.C. Heidrick photo. [81-27-2]

George Robinson's classic photograph of Ocean View Avenue at its peak features the crossovers that shuttled empty cans to the canneries and full cans back over the street to their warehouses. [72-12-53]

THE CANNING PROCESS

Boilermen brought the canneries to life before dawn, firing the huge boilers that would cook the fish and — prior to electrification — provided power to gear drives, link-chain and belt-and-pulley drive equipment throughout the cannery. It was the boilerman who routinely whistled the cannery workers awake to begin their day's toil at the packing tables and canning equipment.

Fish unloaded at the hoppers were pumped ashore by the large turbines in the cannery's pump-house. The fish were then moved by escalator high up into the canneries for California Department of Fish & Game inspection and weighing. Gravity flow from there was used in the process wherever possible.

Cutting that had been traditionally done manually by Chinese and Japanese workers gradually became less specialized by nationality after the introduction of machine cutters. Slotted conveyors in which the sardines were placed were drawn under spinning blades that cut off the heads and tails and eviscerated the fish.

The next stop on the trip to the can was at the packing tables, another conveyor system that moved the prepared fish down a packing line. The famous one-pound oval can — the trademark of Monterey's sardine packing industry — was a curious holdover from the industry's salmon packing origins. Frank Booth, in his early sardine canning experiments, found that five or six Monterey pilchards fit neatly into the oval can. The salmon had passed into the lore of Monterey's early fishpacking years, but left this unique memento of its one-time presidence: it was for this can that the young Knut Hovden had invented the first machine solderer-sealer for Frank Booth.

Cans for the packing lines were often fed down track-like chutes from the floors above to await mating with lids at the sealing machines. Packed cans, depending on the cannery process, might be pre-cooked open before being inverted by machines designed to drain them before sealing. The last step on the way to the sealing machines was usually the addition of tomato sauce, mustard sauce, olive oil or other special seasonings.

Sealed cans were cleaned and loaded into large rolling steel retort baskets, which were then loaded into huge retorts (pressure cookers) to cook *in the cans* for about an hour and a half at approximately fifteen pounds pressure. "The Chef" was a boilerman in overalls, watching and regulating steam pressure and temperatures in the retorts.

Cooling rooms were often provided for the hot cans, often waiting overnight before they could be labeled and fed to "can catchers" for casing up and storage in the warehouses. Each warehouse had box makers who fabricated the cases used by the men catching the cans.

Often cans were cased for storage unlabeled, awaiting the particular order for which they would be labeled. Finally they were loaded into freight cars for the trip down the Southern Pacific tracks to Castroville and the world.

"Locals" on a hopper connected underwater by flexible rubber pipeline to its cannery. Pumps at the canneries literally sucked the sardines ashore for processing.   Donn Clickard photo. [81-41-30]

The huge turbine pumps that sucked the catch ashore from the hoppers delivered them to an escalator system that lifted them to the tops of the canneries for inspection and weighing.   George Robinson photo. [81-21-22]

Rigid inspection by the State of California determined size and condition for processing of sardines for canning and reduction. The street's history is fraught with violation and enforcement actions. Rey Ruppel photo. [80-45-5]

Early hand-cutting of sardines by expert Chinese and Japanese laborers was replaced by short conveyors that drew fish laid in their "slots" under spinning sets of blades that cut off heads and tails. George Robinson photo. [81-21-27]

Cut sardines were then sluiced downstairs to packing lines of women who placed them in a variety of cans. This Fred Harbick photo shows the ladies packing "ovals"—one pound oval cans.   [73-06-6]

Another canning line photo shows ladies packing "talls"—one pound tall, round cans—which became more common in the 1940's. Prior to unionization, these ladies worked as long as it took to can the catch.   Fred Harbick photo. [73-06-7]

Packing a world-famous trademark of Cannery Row—the one pound oval—at Cal Pac. This is the same salmon can for which Knut Hovden invented the sealing machine, launching the Monterey sardine industry. Robinson photo. [81-21-29]

At the end of the packing line there was normally a "repacker" to fill oddly packed cans or repack spilled ones on the conveyor line prior to their trip to the sealing machines.   George Robinson photo. [81-21-31]

Good mechanics were always in demand to keep the high-speed sealing machines functioning properly. Breakdowns were an expensive nemesis to the orderly flow of fish through the canneries.   George Robinson photo. [81-21-30]

Sealed cans of sardines were fed into large rolling bins called "retort baskets," which were wheeled to the cookers where the sardines were literally cooked *in their cans*. Donn Clickard photo. [81-41-9]

The filled retort baskets were then rolled into large horizontal pressure cookers called "retorts" to be cooked by steam pressure.

[74-12-9]

"The Chef" in the sardine cooking process was in reality a boilerman who carefully monitored temperature and steam pressure gauges as the sardines cooked in their cans.   George Robinson photo. [81-21-33]

The human history of Cannery Row is reflected in this 1936 photo of the labeling crew at Hovden's, taking a break on the warehouse loading dock on the Southern Pacific rail line.   [86-61-1]

This Miles Midloch photo of the Hovden crew on a break at the loading dock is a look at old Ocean View Avenue that captures the feeling that John Steinbeck's genius translated into "Cannery Row."   [81-51-2]

REDUCTION AND PROFITS

The relaxation of reduction restrictions brought on by the recession of the early 1920's was a door, once open, that would not close until depletion was a stark reality. H.R. Robbin's early fertilizer production by reduction for Salinas valley agriculture began what was to become first a profitable side-line to canning, and then a separate industry altogether — co-located in most canneries by the forties.

The process was relatively simple and required only modest investment and labor to operate. Its consequences were largely to blame for the stomach wrenching smell blamed on canning of sardines, and an impetus that irrevocably pointed the industry toward suicide. Grinding of offal — fish heads, tails and entrails — and the diversion of increasing tonnage of whole fish accomplished by the industry's legislative lobby, saw otherwise cannable sardines ground into pulp and cooked in screw-cookers before being squeezed of liquid content. The remaining pulp was dried in rotary kilns, and ground into fishmeal. The liquid pressed from the pulp was centrifuged to separate the oil and water, reduced by further cooking to a heavy consistency that was marketed as a poultry feed additive or was added back into the manufacture of "whole" meal fertilizer.

This fishmeal, fertilizer, and other by-product manufacture was far more profitable than sardine canning. In fact, the canning of sardines was ultimately to become a sideline for the reduction and by-product manufacturing process. The sardine industry had lost control of itself in twenty-five years of increased dependence on reduction profits for its survival, a dependence rationalized and disregarded as long as the supply of sardines seemed limitless.

George Robinson provides this look at one of the reduction grinder-dryers that helped turn over two-thirds of the sardines ever landed at Monterey into fishmeal and fertilizer.   [81-21-34]

STEINBECK'S OCEAN VIEW AVENUE

When John Steinbeck wrote *Cannery Row* in New York from memory in 1944, he was recalling and visualizing the street as it existed for him in the mid-thirties. He knew its entire length and many of its inhabitants intimately, having spent much time there in the company of his fascinating friend Ed Ricketts. Steinbeck was living a short distance away on 11th Street in Pacific Grove for the first half of the decade.

It was in this proximity to Cannery Row that John Steinbeck was to finally achieve his first commercial success with *Tortilla Flat*, a success that was also to remove him to the Los Gatos hills. His wife Carol had worked at a number of jobs to support his writing obsession, including working for a time as a secretary for Ed Ricketts' biological supply business, Pacific Biological Laboratories. The move brought her closer to her native San Jose, and it can be said it removed John from his constant companionship with Ed. Their friendship was a powerful and synergistic intellectual interplay that ironically brought a degree of notorious fame to "Doc" with the wartime publication of Steinbeck's nostalgic accounts of life on this peculiar street.

It remains an amazing testimony to John Steinbeck's skill that the worldwide fame and curiosity established by his fiction dealt with a *feeling* of the Row, rather than an explicit physical inventory of it. Through the fortuitous photography of Ted McKay we have a visual overview of Ocean View Avenue as it actually existed. The precise identification of its canneries and landmarks, including those utilized in Steinbeck's fiction, can be accomplished by comparison with the map-guide provided at the conclusion of this book.

John and Carol Steinbeck spent the first half of the 1930's in Pacific Grove; it had drawn Ed Ricketts there in 1923. Lewis Josselyn's photo shows it as they knew it in the thirties.

[71-01-263]

John Steinbeck, to whom old Ocean View Avenue owes a great deal of its worldwide fame as "Cannery Row." His nostalgic account of the street was written from memory in New York in 1944, in a world at war. [81-21-95]

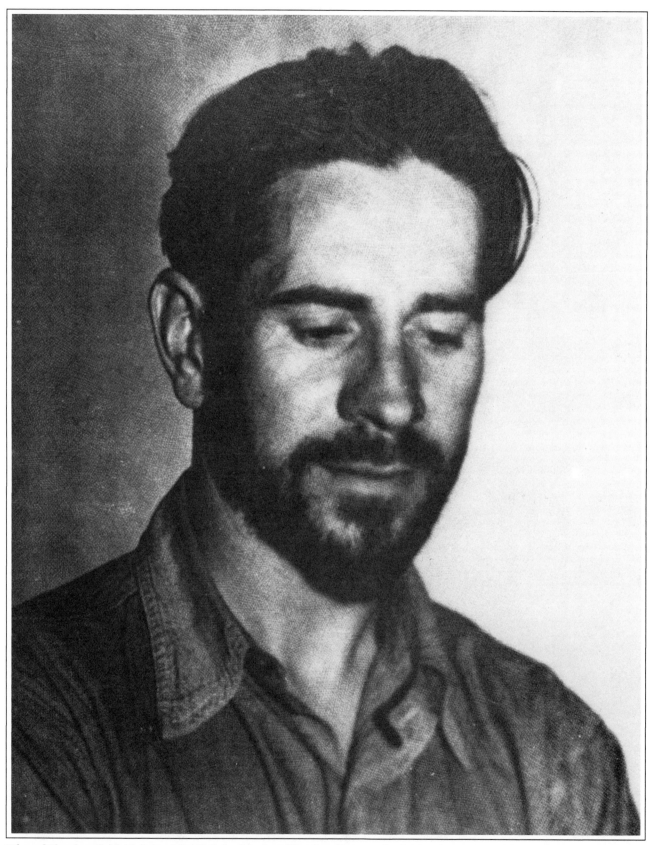

Edward Flanders Robb Ricketts, John Steinbeck's close friend and mentor, had a major impact on modern Marine Biology with his "Between Pacific Tides."

Brian Fitch photo, 1937—Courtesy George Robinson Collection. [81-60-1]

F.E. Booth's cannery, to the right of Fisherman's Wharf in this Ted McKay photo, was the only sardine factory to be permitted in the harbor. Ocean View Avenue begins to the right of this vista. [83-06-18]

"The Street of the Sardine" began at the breakwater with the San Carlos and E.B. Gross canneries in the foreground. The Tevis-Murray estate can still be seen in this photograph from the late 1930's. Ted McKay photo. [83-06-25]

A closer look at the mid-Row from the Tevis-Murray estate to McAbee Beach and the Monterey Canning Company. A comparison to the map-guide index will provide indentification of its other canneries. Ted McKay photo. [80-45-6]

Most of the book *Cannery Row* was written about the neighborhood in this photograph by Ted McKay. Many of the book's locations and landmark's remain, a reward for students of old Ocean View Avenue. [83-06-62]

THE "DOC"

Ed Ricketts is at the epicenter of "Steinbeck's Ocean View Avenue." It is from John's immediate friendship and fascination with Ed's professional, intellectual, philosophical and personal vigor, humor, kindness and compassion that his only slightly fictional accounts of the man flow onto his pages. Nor did Ed object to being a model for John's magic prior to *Cannery Row*.

Professor Richard Astro in *Steinbeck and Ricketts: The Making of a Novelist* illustrates Ed's use as a major character in no less than *six* Steinbeck works. Ed's influence is even recognized by Professor Jackson Benson, the "official" Steinbeck biographer, as having gone far beyond a simple role model. His vision and comprehension had attracted John to begin with, and his involvement with John Steinbeck's growth as a writer was to prove an influence and allegiance that few friendships rival.

Such a man had moved from Chicago, *without* a degree in biology, to set up a biological supply house in Pacific Grove in 1923. His early partnership with A.E. Galigher was soon divided, with Galigher moving his part of the business to Berkeley. Ed became familiar with nearby Cannery Row and its stuttering sardine industry, and no doubt watched with interest as its Murray mansion was threatened by the big oil fire of 1924.

Ricketts' collecting of marine animal species for preparation and shipment to biology classes, colleges, educational and medical researchers continued until his death in 1948 — when his aging car was struck by the Del Monte Express at the Drake Avenue grade-crossing. But *where* he was to conduct this business was fated; he moved his operation into a small building near the Hovden Cannery in 1930.

Across the street from his "Pacific Biological Laboratories" was a house of ill repute, the "Lone Star Cafe," run by a large and respected madam, Flora Woods. Also across the street and closer to Hovden's were the "Wing Chong Market" of Won Yee, and another house of ill repute, the "La Ida Cafe." Directly up the hill from the Lab's front door a triplex for male cannery workers called the "Palace" shared a lot with the old Joss House from China Point. A pretty interesting place, actually.

Into it stepped John Steinbeck after meeting Ed at a party at a friend's house in 1930. That friend, Jack Calvin, with Ritchie Lovejoy and John Steinbeck would struggle and participate in Ed's *Between Pacific Tides*. Ricketts' decade-long development of this book's *then* controversial approach to the study of the inter-relationships of intertidal organisms was unpopular with the head of the Hopkins Marine Station, Dr. Fisher, who fought it until its publication by Stanford in 1939. There are now several generations of senior marine biologists who were inspired into their fields by Ed Ricketts and this book, which *still* remains a major and important influence in its field.

It was to be this decade of the thirties on Ocean View Avenue in this neighborhood where Ed Ricketts lived and worked, to which John Steinbeck gravitated to observe, explore, savor and distill — in the company and stimulation of an unusual talent and intelligence — the stuff that his literary genius is made of. *Cannery Row* by John Steinbeck is Ed's vision and John's genius: it *must* be read for the fullest appreciation of the Cannery Row experience and to appreciate why a writer who did not write history has become inseparable from it.

The Pacific Biological Laboratory of Ed "Doc" Ricketts is the square little building facing the street between the cannery smokestacks in this Ted McKay photo. Across the street in the "Bearflag" of Dora Flood. [84-96-1]

Another not-so-fictional locale from Steinbeck's *Cannery Row* is the area of the frog hunt in Carmel Valley, the entrance to which is seen in this photo of Carmel Valley Road in a slightly later time. [72-03-62]

A great comparison in "Doc's" old neighborhood can be made by contrasting this Fred Harbic photo of the Hovden cannery in the early 1940's with its replacement, the Monterey Bay Aquarium. [76-06-2]

This photo from the Robinson Collection shows Ed Ricketts at work in the Lab with his friend Ritchie Lovejoy, who helped illustrate Ed's *Between Pacific Tides*, still an important work in marine biology. [81-21-70]

This photo by Ed Ricketts Jr. shows a small portion of his father's library inside the Pacific Biological Laboratories. The original Lab was destroyed by fire on November 25, 1936, and rebuilt.   [81-21-71]

Another view inside the Lab by Ed Ricketts Jr. shows Ed's bunk and its hemp rope suspension, with a photograph of a portrait of John Steinbeck by Ellwood Graham on the wall above it—a favorite of Ed's.   [81-21-74]

"The Doc" in a portrait photo thought to be taken shortly after his discharge from the U.S. Army in 1943, the second time he was inducted into military service.

From the Robinson Collection. [81-21-78]

ENCOUNTERING THE LIMITS

The publication of Steinbeck's *Cannery Row* in 1945 coincided with the zenith of Monterey's sardine fishing and canning era, as wartime production enabled its proclamation as "Sardine Capital of the World!" The echos of this proud boast had hardly faded when the Monterey sardine industry and the community it supported were visited by an irony and agony of catastrophic proportions. The 1945-46 season was nearly *half* the volume of the previous year's catch. A stunned industry held its breath and awaited the 1946-47 season: it was to be the worst since 1922! And the 1947-48 season was to be, unbelievably, even worse yet! "Table 8" provides an all-too-vivid picture of the rise and fall of an industry predicated upon the impossible.

POST MORTEM

The honest fear that the worst had really happened was settling in on Monterey. No longer an academic argument between businessmen and biologists, the sardine simply wasn't there for the capture. Ed Ricketts' death was somehow almost symbolic of the unexpected, impossible tragedy for which the cannery barons and fishing families of Monterey were totally unprepared.

Angelo Lucido, Sal Ventimiglia, Knut Hovden and the remaining canners desperately attempted trucking iced fish from the Santa Barbara area. Spoilage, transport costs and insufficient volume doomed such attempts by an industry that had already had its chance to anticipate such contingencies, but had not.

As canneries closed, many into bankruptcy, a ghost town pallor and despair hung heavily over Ocean View Avenue, as strong as the former smell of baking sardine meal. It was going and would soon be gone, this street of the sardine.

The Bearflag was now a concrete warehouse; the La Ida Cafe all but closed. The Wing Chong Market was soon to be liquidated by Won Yee's son, Jack. The filming of the RKO movie "Clash By Night," a production by Louella Parsons' daughter Harriet, could scarcely find enough fish for filming the documentary-like opening scenes of a coastal fishing and canning community. This classic film starred Barbara Stanwyck and introduced Marilyn Monroe, in her co-starring debut — as a *cannery worker* on the cutting machines! — in an industry in its last futile gasps.

TABLE 8
SEASONAL LANDINGS IN TONS
Sardines

Season*	Reduction ships	San Francisco area	Monterey area	Los Angeles area	San Diego area	Total tons
1916–17	----	----	7,710	17,380	2,440	27,530
1917–18	----	70	23,810	41,340	7,360	72,580
1918–19	----	450	35,750	32,530	6,810	75,540
1919–20	----	1,000	43,040	16,580	6,410	67,030
1920–21	----	230	24,960	11,740	1,520	38,450
1921–22	----	80	16,290	19,220	910	36,500
1922–23	----	110	29,210	33,170	2,620	65,110
1923–24	----	190	45,920	35,040	2,780	83,930
1924–25	----	560	67,310	96,330	8,820	173,020
1925–26	----	560	69,010	61,990	5,710	137,270
1926–27	----	3,520	81,860	64,720	2,110	152,210
1927–28	----	16,690	98,020	67,900	4,650	187,260
1928–29	----	13,520	120,290	119,250	1,420	254,480
1929–30	----	21,960	160,050	140,540	2,620	325,170
1930–31	10,960	25,970	109,620	38,490	80	185,120
1931–32	31,040	21,607	69,078	42,656	264	164,645
1932–33	58,790	18,634	89,599	83,605	62	250,690
1933–34	67,820	36,336	152,480	125,047	1,746	383,429
1934–35	112,040	68,477	230,854	178,818	4,865	595,054
1935–36	150,830	76,147	184,470	138,400	10,651	560,498
1936–37	235,610	141,099	206,706	138,115	4,594	726,124
1937–38	67,580	133,718	104,936	109,947	383	416,564
1938–39	43,890	201,200	180,994	146,403	2,800	575,287
1939–40	----	212,453	227,874	96,827	112	537,266
1940–41	----	118,092	165,698	175,592	1,202	460,584
1941–42	----	186,589	250,287	148,912	1,585	587,373
1942–43	----	115,884	184,399	201,510	2,868	504,661
1943–44	----	126,512	213,616	135,311	2,690	478,129
1944–45	----	136,598	237,246	178,294	2,767	554,905
1945–46	----	84,103	145,519	173,110	951	403,683
1946–47	----	2,869	31,391	194,774	4,768	233,802
1947–48	----	94	17,630	101,154	2,463	121,341
1948–49	----	112	47,862	131,830	3,922	183,726
1949–50	----	17,442	131,769	186,433	3,281	338,925
1950–51	----	12,727	33,699	303,752	2,910	353,088
1951–52	----	82	15,897	111,774	1,351	129,104
1952–53	----	----	49	5,635	27	5,711
1953–54	----	----	58	4,111	323	4,492
1954–55	----	----	856	67,099	510	68,465
1955–56	----	----	518	73,943	----	74,461
1956–57	----	----	63	33,564	16	33,643
1957–58	----	----	17	22,255	----	22,272
1958–59	----	----	24,701	79,264	6	103,971
1959–60	----	----	16,109	21,146	1	37,256
1960–61	----	----	2,340	26,436	102	28,878
1961–62	----	----	2,231	23,295	2	25,528
1962–63	----	----	1,211	2,961	----	4,172
1963–64	----	----	1,015	1,895	32	2,942
1964–65	----	----	308	5,717	78	6,103
1965–66	----	----	151	535	33	719
1966–67	----	----	23	311	10	344
1967–68	----	----	10	61	----	71

* Season June through the following May.

Department of Fish and Game, Fish Bulletin No. 149: *The California Marine Fish Catch for 1968 and Historical Review 1916-1968*, by Richard F.G. Heimann and John G. Carlisle, Jr., 1970. A statistical study of disaster.

The Lab, closed after Ed's death, sets the mournful tone for the whole street—which as the "Sardine Capital of the World" was to follow him to a kind of cremation of its own. George Robinson. [81-21-83]

The once bustling "Wing Chong Market" and the sporting "La Ida Cafe" reflect the sad pallor that set in on the whole street as the grim reality of depletion could no longer be disbelieved. George Robinson photo. [81-21-88]

While sardine supplies were holding out further south, desperate canners began trucking fish from southern ports, such as Port Hueneme, to Monterey for processing. [74-12-13]

Trucking of Southern California sardines to Monterey in an effort to save the industry proved unfeasible due to high costs, low volume and heavy spoilage. Absolute disaster had become absolute reality. Fred Harbick photo. [73-06-49]

The 1951-52 season proved to be the worst yet on record as RKO made a film about a coastal fishing and canning town, on location in Monterey. "Clash By Night" remains a near documentary classic, unwittingly recording the demise of the sardine industry at Monterey. Donn Clickard's photo of the filming of a wharfside scene features Barbara Stanwyk on deck with Paul Douglas.   [81-41-27]

Fred Harbick captures the forlorn face of old Ocean View Avenue from the street in front of the La Ida Cafe as "Cannery Row" enters the pale, gray years from which it is only now really recovering. [73-06-2]

Obviously unsuited for other uses, the sardine factories of old Ocean View Avenue seem to stand in the apprehensive silence of a disbelieving ghost town. There will be no more silver harvests here. George Robinson photo. [79-109-1]

FIREY OBITS

The plague of fire was to visit Cannery Row, claiming huge portions of this once indomitable street. Canneries and warehouses, reduction plants and sardine oil storage — an industry soaked in the oily breath of a zillion sardines and caked with the talcum-fine incendiary dust of its fish-meal dependent indulgence — fell easy prey to arsonist and accident. The Sun Gate-West Harbor fire at the former Del Mar Cannery in December 1951 began the fire drill on Ocean View Avenue that would last well into the sixties.

As fate would have it, the once stately Ocean View Hotel of Mr. Wu and Mr. Sam, was to bear silent witness to the funeral pyre of Monterey's once mighty sardine industry, and the dark and unspoken obituary to its blind and suicidal momentum and arrogance.

Farewell to the Old Row, buried by ledgers. Its legacy lies in the mosaic of memories borne by its Alumni.

The Sun Gate-West Harbor fire at the former Del Mar Cannery was reported to be the largest food industry fire in the country's history at the time, estimated at a loss of 1.5 million dollars. William Morgan photo. [78-34-7]

The Sun Gate-West Harbor fire, December 8, 1951, was the first major fire to strike Ocean View Avenue's idled canneries. Both of its cannery warehouses were engulfed in this huge fire. William Morgan photo. [78-34-10]

The same Southern Pacific tracks that pass the nearby site of the original Chinatown witness the revisitation of fire to Ocean View Avenue in this William Morgan photo taken toward Pacific Grove. [78-34-9]

The next major fire, seen from the roof of the aging Ocean View Hotel, claims the Sea Beach Packing Company and the Old Custom House Packing Corporation canneries on October 24, 1953.   William Morgan photo. [78-34-12]

The once proud Ocean View Hotel watched Ocean View Avenue grow and now stoically witnesses its demise. The venerable old hotel escaped fire, but was demolished in 1983, no longer on Ocean View Avenue. William Morgan photo. [78-34-1]

A farewell photo of old Ocean View Avenue five years after the death of Ed Ricketts and the industry, and five years before the street is renamed Cannery Row in honor of John Steinbeck, January 7, 1958.   William Morgan photo, 1953. [78-34-14]

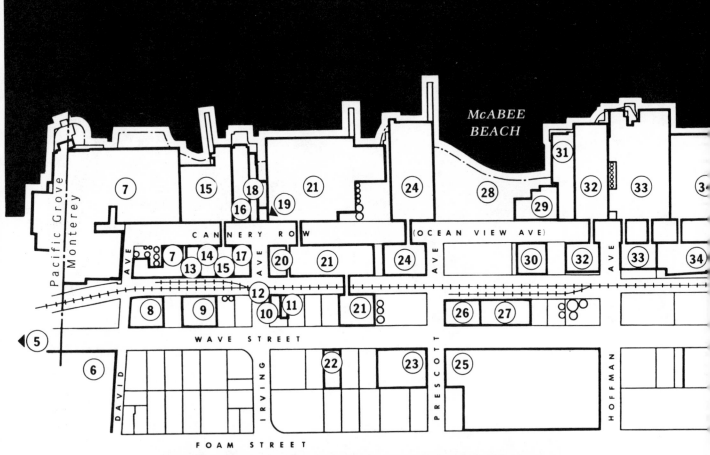

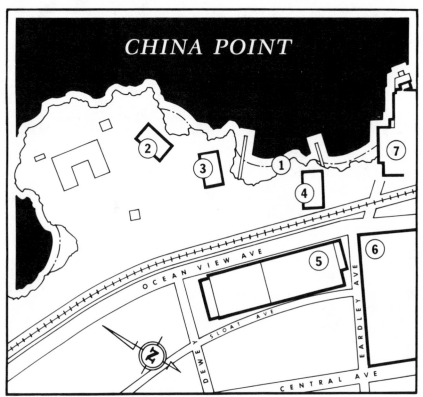

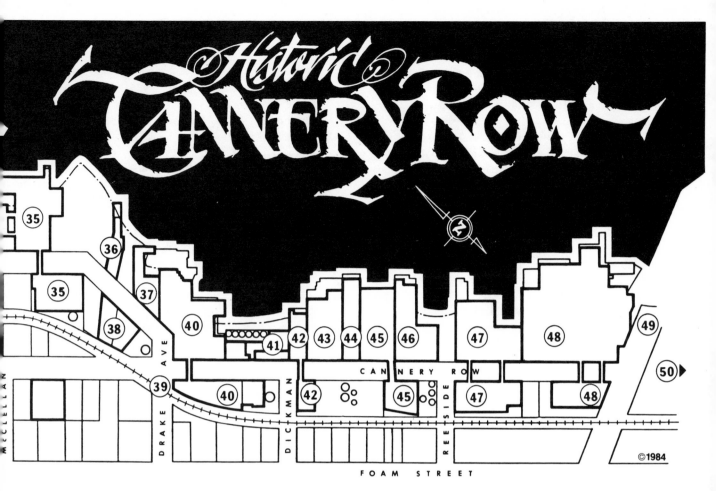

Historic Cannery Row

35
36
35
37
38
40
39
41 42 43 44 45 46 47 48 49
50
CANNERY ROW
40 42 45 47 48
DRAKE AVE
DICKMAN
REESIDE
MCCLELLAN
©1984

FOAM STREET

Map index next page.

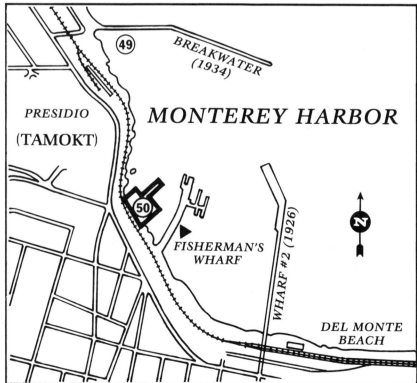

49

BREAKWATER
(1934)

PRESIDIO

(TAMOKT)

MONTEREY HARBOR

50

FISHERMAN'S
WHARF

WHARF #2 (1926)

N

DEL MONTE
BEACH

HISTORICAL MAP-GUIDE INDEX

1. CHINATOWN. 1853-1906. Burned May 6, 1906. Many Chinese move to McAbee Beach and establish another, smaller Chinatown, 1907-1924.
2. HOPKINS MARINE STATION. Originally the Hopkins Seaside Laboratory, located at Lovers Point, Pacific Grove. Moved to China Point in 1915.
3. MONTEREY BOAT WORKS. Established by Pearson and Cochran in 1915. Bought out by Gus Smith circa 1919. Bought by Siino Boatworks in 1937.
4. SIINO BOATWORKS. 1928-1937. Consolidated with Monterey Boatworks in 1937.
5. AMERICAN CAN COMPANY. 1927. Its first manager, Donald E. McDonald, claimed its first year production would be 65,000,000 cans. Closed in 1954.
6. T.A. WORK LUMBERYARD. Established in the early years of cannery construction.
7. HOVDEN FOOD PRODUCTS CORP. 1916-1973. Norwegian-born canning innovator Knut Hovden, left F.E. BOOTH to open his own cannery on New Monterey's *Ocean View Avenue.* Burns August 11, 1921 and was rebuilt. Reduction plant blaze October 5, 1924 lasts two days. "The King of Cannery Row" retired in 1951. Site of the Monterey Bay Aquarium.
8. McFADDEN'S, now known as the "OLD COAST HOUSE." A canning era home and boarding house.
9. FISHMEAL BARN above the tracks, behind the WING CHONG MARKET—the model for John Steinbeck's "Palace Flophouse" in *Cannery Row.* (See lower photo, page 103.)
10. "PALACE FLOPHOUSE" in its actual location as a triplex for single cannery workers, sharing a small lot with the CHINESE JOSS HOUSE. *Cannery Row,* Chapters 1 and 7.
11. CHINESE JOSS HOUSE. Demolished on this site in the early 1940's, sharing the lot with the "Palace Flophouse."
12. "CHICKEN WALK" in *Cannery Row.* Planks up the embankment from the tracks to the unfinished Irving Avenue.
13. LA IDA CAFE. 1929. One of the Row's "houses of ill repute." *Cannery Row.* Chapter 7.
14. WING CHONG MARKET. Won Yee and eleven Chinese Investors open a grocery and dry-goods store, September 1918. *Cannery Row,* Chapter 1.
15. SEA PRIDE PACKING CO. Replaces Great Western Sardine Co. in 1925. Sells to a New York firm, ATLANTIC COAST FISHERIES, in December 1945. Cannery burns in 1980.
16. MONTEREY FISH PRODUCTS. Established in 1915 by "reduction" pioneer, Max Schaefer.
17. "VACANT LOT" and BLACK CYPRESS of *Cannery Row,* Introduction and Chapter 1. Location of MALLOY'S BOILER, Chapter 8.
18. DEL VISTA PACKING CO. 1946. A late entry into the reduction business.
19. PACIFIC BIOLOGICAL LABORATORIES. 1929. Edward F. "Doc" Ricketts moved his biological supply business from Pacific Grove. Appears as "Western Biological Laboratory" in *Cannery Row,* Chapters 5, 10, 20, 21 and 30. A private men's club since 1957.
20. FLORA WOOD'S LONE STAR CAFE. 1923-1941. The "Bear Flag Restaurant" of "Dora Flood"—the Row's most notorious bordello and its most magnanimous madam—Chapters 3 and 16 of *Cannery Row.* Flora dies penniless on August 1, 1948.
21. BAYSIDE FISH AND FLOUR CO. 1916. Became Cypress Canning Company, September, 1927. Became DEL MAR CANNING CO. on January 26, 1928. A major fire on November 25, 1936 also destroys Ed "Doc" Ricketts' Lab. Both are rebuilt. Burns as SUN GATE-WEST HARBOR on December 8, 1951.
22. MOW WO'S. A Chinese grocery and hardware store established in the early 1920's.
23. AURORA HALL. An early 1920's YMCA, Portuguese Hall, boxing ring and cannery worker's cafeteria.
24. MONTEREY CANNING CO. 1918. Constructed on the site of the Chinese "Monterey Fish Canning Co." (1910-1916) by Scotchmen George Harper, and A.M. Allen—partner in the Point Lobos abalone cannery.
25. UNION SUPPLY COMPANY. Lumber mill and yard owned by Henry Hansen. Now a municipal parking lot.
26. F.E. BOOTH REDUCTION PLANT. Construction begins October 2, 1917 as Booth's late entry into large-scale fishmeal and fertilizer production. It could not be located with his cannery in the harbor.
27. EDGEWATER PACKING CO. Added to the old F.E. Booth reduction plant circa 1940.

28. McABEE BEACH. An early Portuguese shore-whaling station from the 1860's, named for the Scot whose beach cottages and boat rental replaced whaling from this beach near the turn of the century. Many Chinese relocated to this site, leased to them by McAbee after the fire at China Point in 1906.

29. OCEAN VIEW HOTEL. 1927-1983. Built and owned by Mr. and Mrs. Maen Chang Wu on part of the McABEE BEACH CHINATOWN site (1907-1924).

30. MARINA APARTMENTS. 1929. An annex to the Ocean View Hotel built by Mr. Wu and Mr. Sam. It became an "institution of commercialized love."

31. SEA BEACH PACKING CO. Groundbreaking in September, 1945. Burns in 1953.

32. OLD CUSTOM HOUSE PACKING CORPORATION. 1929-1952. Closes in November 1952. Burns in October 1953.

33. CARMEL CANNING CO. 1918-1962. Ben Senderman retires, selling his new cannery to local investors. It burns in 1967.

34. MONTEREY FISHING AND CANNING CO. 1902. Harry Malpas builds the first cannery on the New Monterey coastline, backed by Japanese investment. It becomes PACIFIC FISH CO. in August, 1908—the first *major* canning operation on what was to become Cannery Row. It was bought by CALIFORNIA PACKING CORP. on March 1, 1926. Closes in April, 1962. Burns in 1967 and 1973.

35. SAN XAVIER CANNING CO. 1917. Frank Raiter's "San X" cannery burns in 1967. Its reduction plant remains.

36. WESTERN SARDINE CO. Construction begins on this reduction plant in December, 1945.

37. THE FERRANTE CO. Built by Sal Ferrante, son-in-law of Pietro Ferrante, in 1945.

38. Early addresses of Ben Senderman and the Hovdens. Perhaps constructed as support houses for the TEVIS-MURRAY ESTATE, near the turn of the century.

39. SITE OF ED "DOC" RICKETTS' COLLISION with the evening Del Monte Express, May 8, 1948. Born May 14, 1897; he dies May 11, 1948. Steinbeck details the tragedy as part of "About Ed Ricketts," the preface to *The Log From the Sea of Cortez.* 1951.

40. OXNARD CANNING CO. Sal Ferrante builds this huge cannery in *five months,* opening in October, 1942.

36-44. TEVIS-MURRAY ESTATE. 1901-1944. Hugh Tevis died on his honeymoon; the palatial estate built for his bride was then sold to James A. Murray in 1904. The estate occupied nearly 1,000 feet of Monterey's scenic coastline (sites 36 through 44). After its sale in late 1940, it became canneries and reduction plants.

41. WESTERN FISH PROCESSORS. July 1943. A "stick-water" (waste water) treatment plant that reduced liquid canning "waste" into concentrated by-products, accompanied by horrendous odor.

42. AENEAS SARDINE PACKING CO. 1945. Its cannery-to-warehouse "cross-over" is one of only two originals left on The Row. Like many late entries to the industry, it was to be the victim of poor timing.

43. CENTRAL PACKING CO. A reduction plant constructed on the Tevis Estate site.

44. RONADA FISHERIES and MAGNOLIA PACKING CO. Late 1940's entries into the reduction process.

45. ENTERPRISE PACKERS. The warehouse building remains of this cannery, constructed in 1945 during World War II demand and just preceeding the disappearance of the sardines.

46. CALIFORNIA FISHERIES CO. 1916. A Japanese export firm destroyed by the oil tank fire of September, 1924. Sal Ventimiglia builds CALIFORNIA FROZEN FISH CO. on the vacant site in 1945.

47. E.B. GROSS CANNING CO. 1919-1943. Destroyed by the 1924 oil tank fire and rebuilt. Ed Gross sells in 1943 to PENINSULA PACKING CO.

48. SAN CARLOS CANNING CO. 1927. Angelo Lucido headed this major cannery that was owned by boatowners and fishermen. It burns on Thanksgiving, 1956.

49. COALINGA OIL AND TRANSPORTATION PIER. 1904. Also known as the Associated Oil Company Pier, this 650-foot pier was destroyed by the oil fire of 1924. Monterey's BREAKWATER was constructed on its location. 1934.

50. F.E. BOOTH CO. 1903-1941. In 1903, Booth buys out his competitor H.R. Robbin's rudimentary plant and expands it into the first major canning operation of Monterey's sardine era. "The Father of the Sardine Industry" is forced out of business in 1941 by fellow cannery owners who help ensure that his municipal lease in the harbor is not renewed. He closes May 28, 1941. He dies December 12, 1941.

RECOMMENDED READING
ABOUT STEINBECK/CANNERY ROW

Astro, Richard. *John Steinbeck and Edward Ricketts: The Shaping of a Novelist.* Minneapolis: University of Minnesota Press, 1973.

Benson, Jackson J. *The True Adventures of John Steinbeck, Writer.* New York: Viking Press, 1984.

Elstob, Winston. *Chinatown. A Legend of Old Cannery Row.* Berkeley: Condor's Sky Press, 1965.

Hedgepeth, Joel, ed. *The Outer Shores.* (Two volumes). Eureka: Mad River Press, 1978.

Lydon, Sandy. *CHINESE GOLD: The Chinese and the Monterey Bay Region.* Capitola: Capitola Book Company, 1985.

Mangelsdorf, Tom. *A History of Steinbeck's Cannery Row.* Santa Cruz: Western Tanager Press, 1986.

McGlynn, Betty Hoag. "Casa de Las Olas" (House of the Waves; the Tevis-Murray Estate). *Noticias del Puerto de Monterey* (Quarterly bulletin of the Monterey History and Art Association), Vol XXVI, No. 2, June, 1985, and No. 3, September, 1985.

Reinstedt, Randy. *Where Have All the Sardines Gone?* Carmel: Ghost Town Publications, 1978.

Weber, Tom. *Cannery Row, A Time to Remember.* Orenda/Unity Press. 1983.

BY JOHN STEINBECK

Cannery Row. New York: Viking Press, 1945.

Log From the Sea of Cortez. (Containing the preface "About Ed Ricketts") New York: Viking Press, 1951.

Sweet Thursday. (The sequel to Cannery Row) New York: Viking Press, 1954.

BY EDWARD F. RICKETTS

Ricketts, Edward F., and Jack Calvin. *Between Pacific Tides.* Stanford: Stanford University Press, 1939. Fourth Edition, 1968.

"The Row"

A street with every right
to be dead . . .
and odds that it should be
were it not for the
Steinbeck in all of it.
An incomplete demise
of a way of life and another time
perhaps better truly dead
than irreverenced . . .

Michael K. Hemp